CRIBBAGE

How to Play and Win

Frank and Simon Buttler

After more than three hundred years since it was first described, cribbage remains one of the best card games for two or more players. This books is in two parts, the first introduces the game to those who have never played it before and the second, and much larger part, explains the intricacies of the game to more experienced players and gives guidance to improve the chances of winning.

The book describes both the six-card and the five-card games in detail and how to obtain advantage from any of the countless card combinations, which could be received during play. Numerous examples are included, each with its own commentary and checked by computer programs. The examples are written in easily understood tabular form and have been chosen to illustrate the subtleties of each stage of the game.

The title of the book, *Cribbage — How to Play and Win*, summarises its aims. The game is great fun to play and you will enjoy it, whether you win or lose. As enjoyment increases with winning, so this book, by enabling you to win more often, will magnify your enjoyment and enhance your pleasure!

CRIBBAGE

How to Play and Win

Frank and Simon Buttler

WEIDENFELD & NICOLSON
in association with
PETER CRAWLEY

First published in Great Britain 2000
in association with Peter Crawley
by Victor Gollancz
3rd impression 2013

This edition published 2014
in association with Peter Crawley
by Weidenfeld & Nicolson
an imprint of the Orion Publishing Group Ltd
Orion House, 5 Upper St Martin's Lane
London WC2H 9EA

An Hachette UK Company

1 2 3 4 5 6 7 8 9 10

A CIP catalogue record for this book is available from the British Library.

ISBN: 978 0 297 87113 2

Printed and bound by CPI Group (UK) Ltd, Croydon, CR0 4YY

The Orion Publishing Group's policy is to use papers that are natural, renewable and recyclable products and made from wood grown in sustainable forests. The logging and manufacturing processes are expected to conform to the environmental regulations of the country of origin.

www.orionbooks.co.uk

Contents

INTRODUCTION

Although the origins of the game of cribbage are not known with certainty, it is generally agreed to have developed from an earlier game called Noddy. The invention of cribbage as it is known today is often accredited to Sir John Suckling, an English nobleman who lived from 1609 to 1642 and who inherited a fortune from his father in 1627. He was a favourite at court and was described as having a sparkling wit and as being the greatest gallant of his time. During his lifetime he was famous as a playwright and a poet, and a few of his poems remain popular to this day. In 1641 he was involved in a plot to rescue the Earl of Stafford from imprisonment in the Tower of London. When the plot was discovered he fled to France and a year later, having lost his fortune, he took poison and died.

An account of the life of Sir John Suckling was included by John Aubrey, the historian and gossip, in his "Brief Lives"[1]. Aubrey's account, written some time after Suckling's death, is largely based on the recollections of friends and particularly those of Sir William Davenant. The account states that Sir John invented the game of "cribbidge" and that "he was the greatest gamester, both for bowling and cards" and that "he played at cards rarely well, and did use to practise by himself a bed, and there studyed how the best way of managing the cards could be". Irrespective of whether or not the full credit for inventing cribbage should be given to Sir John Suckling, the fact remains that the game was well established by 1674 when its rules, little different from those used today were published by Charles Cotton in "The Compleat Gamester"[2] and, after more than three hundred years, cribbage remains one of the most popular card games for two players.

The majority of card games belong to one of two types, those which involve the taking of tricks, such as whist or bridge, and those where sets of cards are collected during the game, such as rummy, canasta, bezique or piquet. Cribbage does not belong to either of these types and the cards are used in a more numerical way than in most other games. In many ways the game is an exercise in mental arithmetic.

In cribbage each player tries to be the first to score a set number of points, these being awarded in several different ways and gathered during the course of the game in small increments. Several deals are required in order to complete a game. In its original form the players both received five cards at each deal, hence the name five-card cribbage, and this game is still played. In the nineteenth century, however, a new form was introduced in which each player was dealt six cards, hence the name six-card cribbage. The latter is now more widely played because, with an extra card, points are scored more rapidly and therefore at first sight the game appears to be more exciting. This is not entirely true and, although neither game is particularly difficult to play, the original five-card game needs more skill in order to play it well. With very slight variations the same rules apply to both the five- and six-card games.

Almost all books of card games give both the basic rules of cribbage and give an indication of how the game should be played. A few books also give detailed guidance on the tactics that can be used in order to improve the chance of winning. Notable amongst these are those by Bohn[3] and Hoyle[4] in the nineteenth century and, more recently, those by Anderson[5] and Wergin[6]. The advice given in such books is largely based on the practical experience gained after playing countless games of cribbage. They describe how a player should use the cards received to try to gain the most points for himself and to restrict the points obtained by his opponent. The same is true for the advice given in this book, most of which is based on the practical experience of the authors. In addition, however, this book includes a more mathematical examination of the cards received which not only checks upon the knowledge obtained by experience but also allows guidelines to be developed which assist the players in using their cards in the most beneficial manner.

The first parts of this book are designed to introduce the game to those who have never played it before and to act as a reminder to those who have only played infrequently. Each stage of the game is described separately, together with general advice on how it should be played. The standard rules of the game follow the main parts of the text but should be referred to when necessary as it is important that the proper rules should be followed by all cribbage players, irrespective of their ability. A glossary of terms is included because cribbage, like other games which have developed over a long period of time, uses a number of unusual terms.

Although most frequently played by two, cribbage is also popular for three or four players. Descriptions of both the three-handed and four-handed versions are included and advice is given on the additional skills required to play them well. They are both very enjoyable games.

The later chapters of the book have been written to give advice, to both the learner and the more experienced player, on the best way of obtaining the maximum advantage from the many millions of card combinations which could be received from the dealer in either the five- or the six-card game. In the former three cards from five, and in the latter four cards from six, have to be selected as the cards to be retained as the hand. Computer programs have been written to calculate which cards should be retained as the hand in order to have the best chance of scoring points from a given deal. By analysing the results from the programs it has been possible to develop guidelines which simplify the selection procedure and enable the player to check and expand the knowledge he has gained by experience.

The tables in this book contain examples from the many deals examined and have been selected to cover most of the types of card combinations which could be received by either player in the course of a game. The comments made for each of these examples form the basis of the overall guidelines of the selection procedures which have been developed and described in the later chapters. These aim to help a player to win by using the most suitable tactics at each stage of the game. The numerical results from the programs which are given in the tables are only included for the purpose of illustration and to corroborate the advice given in the text. Complex calculations during a game of cribbage are inappropriate.

References

1. Aubrey, John. *Brief Lives chiefly of Contemporaries set down by John Aubrey between the years 1669 and 1696*, edited by the Rev. Andrew Clark for the Clarendon Press in 1898.

2. Cotton, Charles. *The Compleat Gamester*. Printed by A.M. for R.Cutler and to be sold by Henry Brome at the Gun at the West-end of St.Pauls, London, 1674.

3. Bohn, Henry G. *The Hand-book of Games*, pub. Henry G.Bohn, York Street, Covent Garden, London, 1850.

4. *The American Hoyle; or Gentleman's Hand-book of Games*, 13th ed. pub. Dick and Fitzgerald, New York, 1880.

5. Anderson, Douglas. *All About Cribbage*, pub. Bailey Bros., Folkestone, England, 1974.

6. Wergin, Joseph P. *Win at Cribbage*, pub. Oldcastle Books, 18 Coleswood Road, Harpenden, Herts. AL5 1EQ. 1993

Chapter 1

HOW TO PLAY

Object of the Game

Cribbage is usually a game for two but it can also be played by three or four. The winner is the first to obtain a set number of points and, although there are slight differences between the rules for the two-, three- and four-handed games, the main rules for obtaining the points are the same for each. A complete pack of 52 cards is used and the four suits are equivalent to each other. The cards have their numerical face values, with Ace counting 1, except for the court cards which are all given the value of 10.

Card	K	Q	J	10	9	8	7	6	5	4	3	2	A
Value	10	10	10	10	9	8	7	6	5	4	3	2	1

Points are awarded in a number of ways, the most important being:

(a) for combinations of cards whose numerical sum adds up to 15, (e.g., 9 + 6, K + 5),

(b) for cards of the same numerical rank, (e.g., two kings, three sixes), and

(c) for runs of three or more cards in sequence (e.g., A + 2 + 3, 7 + 8 + 9 + 10).

The full details of all the different ways in which points can be obtained are given later.

The game is completed when a set number of points has been scored and, in order to achieve this, the cards have to be dealt several times before a player can reach the required number and win the game. The cards must be dealt and played according to an agreed procedure which is divided into a number of stages. The procedure for two-handed six-card cribbage is described here as this is the form of the game which is now most widely played.

Stages in the game

1. The Cut

The players cut the pack to select the dealer of the first hand. The player cutting the lowest card, Ace counting low, becomes the first dealer. Subsequently the deal alternates between the players.

2. The Deal

The dealer shuffles the cards, the non-dealer cuts the pack and, starting with the non-dealer, the cards are dealt face down until both players have six cards. The remaining cards, called the stockpile, are placed face down between the players.

3. The Hand and the Crib

After examining the cards, each player decides which four to keep and discards the other two, face down, into the crib. The crib always belongs to the dealer. The cards in the crib must not be exposed until the cards retained by the players as their hands have been played and scored.

4. The 'Turn-Up' Card

The non-dealer cuts the stockpile, the dealer takes the top card from the bottom portion and places it face up on top of the stockpile. This card is called the 'Turn-Up' card or the 'Starter'.

5. The Play

The non-dealer selects one of the cards retained in hand and, placing it face up on the table, announces its numerical value. The dealer then does likewise and states the numerical sum of both the cards. Cards continue to be played alternately until either the sum of the cards equals 31 or until a card cannot be played without the sum exceeding 31. When unable to play a card without the total exceeding 31, a player says 'Go'. The opponent must continue playing until either 31 is reached or until unable to do so and then also says 'Go'. The process is repeated, the count starting at zero again, with the lead changing to the player who did not play the last card in the previous sum. Play continues in this way until all eight cards from the two hands have been played. The player of the last card in each sum scores 2 points if it equals 31 and 1 point when the sum is less than 31.

During this stage of the game points are also scored when the sum of the cards played equals 15, when cards are paired and when sequences of cards are formed. Details of this are given in the section dealing with scoring.

6. The Showing

Each player then places the cards from hand face up so that the opponent can see them and announces all the scoring combinations in conjunction with the 'Turn-Up' card. The points from the non-dealer are recorded first. After scoring the points from the hand the dealer turns over the four cards in the crib and, again using the 'Turn-Up' card, declares the points scored from them. The formal manner in which the score is announced is described later.

Several deals are required before either player can gain sufficient points to complete the game. The deal alternates between the two players, the same sequences of play applying to each deal.

Method of Scoring

Each player keeps a running tally of the points scored and this is generally done by using a wooden cribbage board. Any points obtained must be pegged on to the cribbage board as they are scored, otherwise they are lost. Traditionally the board has, for each player, two parallel rows of 30 holes, marked in groups of 5, plus one game hole. Each player uses two pegs to show both the individual points scored and the cumulative score as the game progresses. In addition the board sometimes has extra holes so that a record can be kept of the games won. For five-card two-handed cribbage the game ends when 61 points have been scored, i.e., once round the board and into the game hole. Six-card two-handed cribbage is now more popular and for this the game ends at a score of 121, i.e., twice round the board and into the game hole. Some modern cribbage boards have, for each player, a continuous track of 120 holes marked in groups of 5, and a game hole with extra holes for the games won.

1. Points scored by chance

If the 'Turn-Up' card is a Jack the dealer scores 2 points. This is generally called 'Two for His Heels'. All other points, apart from penalties, are scored either as the cards are played or from the counts from the hands and crib in combination with the 'Turn-Up' card.

2. Points scored during play

(a) 2 points are scored by the player making the sum of the cards played equal to 15.
(b) 2 points are scored by the player making the sum of the cards played equal to 31.
(c) 1 point is scored by the player of the last card when both players have said 'Go', neither player having in their hand a card which would bring the score to 31.
(d) 2 points are scored by pairing the previous card played.
(e) 6 points are scored by the player of the last card when three cards of the same rank (e.g., three Queens) are played consecutively without the sum exceeding 31. (Because three cards of the same rank can be paired in three different ways, the score of 6 derives from the 2 points for each pairing).
(f) 12 points are scored by the player of the last card when four cards of the same rank (e.g., four sixes) are played consecutively without the score exceeding 31. (Because four cards of the same rank can be paired in six different ways, the score of 12 derives from the 2 points for each pairing).
(g) 1 point for each card in a sequence. The sequence, or sequences, must occur within the same count to 31. Note that the cards must be played consecutively but not necessarily in order of rank. Thus three cards could be played, for example, in the order 6, 7, 8 or 6, 8, 7 or 7, 6, 8 or 7, 8, 6 or 8, 6, 7 or 8, 7, 6 and three points would be scored whatever the order. A sequence can contain more than three cards and sequences of four or five cards are fairly common.

3. Points scored from the hand in combination with the 'Turn-Up' card

After the cards have been played the players pick up their own cards and calculate the points scored from them in combination with the 'Turn-Up' card. The non-dealer is the first to score and to peg the points obtained.

(a) 2 points are awarded for each way in which the sum of 15 can be made. There are many ways in which this can be done.
(i) Two-card combinations, e.g., (K + 5), (Q + 5), (J + 5), (10 + 5), (9 + 6), (8 + 7).
(ii) Three-card combinations, e.g., (K + 4 + A), (K + 3 + 2), (9 + 4 + 2), (8 + 4 + 3), etc.
(iii) Four-card combinations, e.g., (Q + 2 + 2 + A), (8 + 4 + 2 + A), (7 + 4 + 3 + A), etc.
(iv) Five-card combinations, e.g., (5 + 4 + 3 + 2 + A), (6 + 3 + 3 + 2 + A), etc.

(b) Cards of the same rank
(i) 2 points for a pair of cards of the same rank, e.g., (Q + Q), (4 + 4), etc.
(ii) 6 points for three cards of the same rank, e.g., (J + J + J), (2 + 2 + 2), etc.

Such combinations are called 'Pairs Royal'; three cards of the same rank can be paired in three different ways, each scoring 2 points, giving a total of 6 points.
(iii) 12 points for four cards of the same rank, e.g., (3 + 3 + 3 + 3), etc.

Such combinations are called 'Double Pairs Royal'; four cards can be paired in six different ways, each scoring 2 points, giving a total of 12 points.

(c) 4 points are scored if all the cards in the hand are of the same suit (four-card flush) and 5 points if the cards in hand and the 'Turn-Up' card are of the same suit (five-card flush).

(d) 1 point is scored for each card in a sequence. Points are scored for every sequence in the hand as well as those for pairs as described in (b). Thus—
(i) 3 points for a single sequence of three cards (8 + 9 + 10), and 4 points for a single sequence of four cards (8 + 9 + 10 + J), etc. Note that although a four-card sequence consists of two three-card sequences (8 + 9 + 10 and 9 + 10 + J) it only scores 4 and not 6 points.
(ii) 8 points for four-card combinations, such as (8 + 9 + 9 + 10), which contain two sequences, each of three cards, and one pair of cards. 2 x 3 + 2 = 8.
(iii) 10 points for five-card combinations, such as (8 + 9 + 9 + 10 + J), which contain two sequences, each of four cards, and one pair of cards. 2 x 4 + 2 = 10.
(iv) 15 points for five-card combinations, such as (5 + 6 + 6 + 6 + 7), which contain three sequences, each of three cards, and three pairs of cards. 3 x 3 + 3 x 2 = 15.
(v) 16 points for five-card combinations, such as (5 + 5 + 6 + 7 + 7), which contain four sequences, each of three cards, and two pairs of cards. 4 x 3 + 2 x 2 = 16.

(e) 1 point if a Jack, held in the hand, is of the same suit as the 'Turn-Up' card. This is called 'One for His Nob'.

4. Points scored from the crib in combination with the 'Turn-Up' card

The method of scoring points from the crib follows exactly the same pattern as that used for the hands. The only exception is that most players do not count points for a *four-card flush* from the crib, possibly because it is pure chance for the discards from the players to be of the same suit, whereas, for the cards kept in the hand, a conscious decision is necessary in order to retain four of the same suit. It is therefore rather paradoxical that a *five-card flush* in the crib is allowed and scores five points.

5. Points scored from penalties

Whether or not penalty points are awarded depends on how seriously the players regard the game. Many players ignore penalties as they are unlikely to contribute much to the overall score. Because of this the points from penalties are dealt with in a separate section.

SCORING SYSTEM

	The Play (points)	The Hand (points)	The Crib (points)
'31' (sum of the count during play equals 31)	2		
'Go' (sum of the count during play is less than 31)	1		
'Two for his Heels' ('Turn-Up' card is a Jack)	2		
Fifteen-two (15/2) (two or more cards totalling 15)	2	2	2
Two cards of the same rank (pair)	2	2	2
Three cards of the same rank ('Pairs Royal')	6	6	6
Four cards of the same rank ('Double Pairs Royal')	12	12	12
Three or more cards in numerical sequence	1 point per card	1 point per card	1 point per card
'One for His Nob' (Jack same suit as 'Turn-Up' card)		1	1
Four cards in same suit (Four-card flush)		4	0
Five cards in same suit (Five-card flush)		5	5

Announcing the scores

At each stage of the game the scores are announced in a ritualistic manner, the same system being used as the cards are played and when the scores from the hands and the crib are calculated. This has the advantage that each player can check on the points claimed by the opponent. If mistakes are made they can be rectified and, if desired, penalised. All of the individual points are stated together with their continuous cumulative score. It is usual to start with combinations which add up to 15, stating all of them in turn, and then to state the points derived from pairs and sequences and to finish with any other scoring combinations which are allowed. The following examples of various hands are included to illustrate the method of announcing the points scored.

In each of the examples the 'Turn-Up' card is shown in bold type and the cumulative score, and the card combinations from which it is derived, are shown in italics.

1. Hand and 'Turn-Up' card consists of (5 + J + Q + K) and **K**.

The score is announced as follows:
Fifteen two (5 + J),
fifteen four (5 + Q),
fifteen six (5 + K),
fifteen eight (5 + ***K****),*
two is ten (K + ***K****),*
three is thirteen (J + Q + K),
three is sixteen (J + Q + ***K****).*
Total = 16.

2. Hand and 'Turn-Up' card consisting of (A + 2 + 2 + 3) and **Q**.

The score is announced as follows:
Fifteen two (A + 2 + 2 + ***Q****),*
fifteen four (2 + 3 + ***Q****),*
fifteen six (2 + 3 + ***Q****),*
two is eight (2 + 2),
three is eleven (A + 2 + 3),
three is fourteen (A + 2 + 3).
Total = 14.

3. Hand and 'Turn-Up' card all of the same suit and consisting of (4 + 5 + 6 + 9) and **J**.

The score is announced as follows:
Fifteen two (4 + 5 + 6),
fifteen four (5 + J),
fifteen six (9 + 6),
three is nine (4 + 5 + 6),
five for a flush is fourteen.
Total = 14.

4. Hand and 'Turn-Up' card consisting of (5 + 5 + 6 + J) and **2**. J and 2 of the same suit.

The score is announced as follows:
Fifteen two (5 + J),
fifteen four (5 + J),
two is six (5 + 5),
'One for His Nob' is seven.
Total = 7.

Chapter 2

STRATEGY AND TACTICS

There is an element of chance in all games of cards and cribbage is no exception. However to play cribbage well requires considerable skill and there is a significant increase in the probability of winning if careful thought is given to the overall strategy and the tactics to use at each stage of the game. Although the strategy may not change greatly, it is likely that the tactics used will vary as the game proceeds and, because the best tactics for one part of the game may not always be the wisest for another, each stage of the game will be considered separately. The relative importance of each stage for scoring points, and the risks involved, can then be more fully appreciated.

For each deal the total number of points which can be gained depends both on chance, that is the cards the players receive, and the abilities of both players to maximise their own score and to minimise their opponent's. Because the cards will be dealt about nine times for each game, and several games are likely to be played, the element of chance will tend to balance out. It is therefore the difference in the players' abilities to use their cards fully which has most influence on the outcome.

The Cut for First Deal

For two-handed six-card cribbage the winner of each game is the first to peg 121 points. With the exception of the few points which may be scored for penalties, all the points in each game come from pegging as the cards are played and from the counts in the hands and cribs. Records have shown that, averaging the points for each deal, the dealer scores a total of 16 points and the non-dealer 10. On the basis of average scores the winner of the cut will be dealer on five occasions and non-dealer for four, and should gain 120 points, and be within 1 point of winning the game. (5 x 16) + (4 x 10) = 120 points. The loser of the cut will be non-dealer five times and dealer for four and, on the basis of average scores, should gain 114 points. (5 x 10) + (4 x 16) = 114 points.

It is clear, therefore, that for a single game the player winning the cut and dealing first has a distinct advantage. To try to eliminate this imbalance it is usual, when more than one game is played, for the starting deal to alternate between the players. The winner of one game should not be the first dealer in the next, contrary to the way some play.

At first sight the difference between 114 and 120 may not appear to be significant but, for the majority of games, it is the difference between winning and losing. To try to overcome this imbalance many players, at the beginning of each game, tend to take slightly greater risks in discarding to the crib and in playing the cards when they are the non-dealer. The reverse is true for the dealer of the first hand who will take few risks in order to protect the advantage of the imbalance. A detailed discussion of the problems involved in discarding to the crib is given in a later section.

The importance of the position held at the last deal of the game

The total number of points for a player to be in a winning position in the final stages of the game can be affected by the order in which the players record their points on the cribbage board. For each deal the non-dealer is always the first to score and record the count from the hand. On the basis of average scores, and after eight deals with each player being dealer on four occasions, both will have scored 104 points. (4 x 16) + (4 x 10) = 104.

After the cards have been dealt for the ninth time it is immaterial how many points the dealer has in hand and crib if the non-dealer, by pegging as the cards are played and from the count from hand, can score the required 17 points to win the game. This is unlikely. However, if gaining, on average, one extra point per deal for the first eight deals, the non-dealer has a total of 112 points and, on the basis of average scores, is likely to score the required 9 points to win the game. Both players should, therefore, be mindful of the importance of the position held at the end game and, unless it is necessary to change tactics, the dealer of the first hand should play the cards with caution in order to try to prevent the opponent from scoring some of the extra points which could produce a winning position.

The relative importance of the points from the play, the hand and the crib

As mentioned above a detailed examination of the points awarded from a great many games of two-handed six-card cribbage has shown that, on average for each deal, the dealer scores a total of 16 and the non-dealer 10. The breakdown of the scores into those from pegging as the cards are played and the count from the hands and crib is as follows:

	Dealer	Non-dealer
Points pegged during play	3.5	2.5
Points scored from hand	8.0	7.5
Points scored from crib	4.5	0.0
Total	16.0	10.0

Note the differences in the scores obtained by the dealer and the non-dealer for pegging as the cards are played and from their hands. There are a number of reasons for the differences. The non-dealer is always the first to lead and is often forced to lead a card which enables the dealer to score 15/2 with the second card played. In addition, because ‘Go’ and ‘31’ are often reached after four cards have been played, the non-dealer, as leader, is less likely to score such points. There is also the chance of the dealer scoring ‘Two for His Heels’, and these reasons result in the dealer, on average, gaining one extra point per deal from the points pegged during play. In contrast, it is somewhat surprising that there is, on average, only half a point difference between the dealer’s and non-dealer’s scores from their hands. The non-dealer always tries to discard so that there is the least advantage to the opponent’s crib. However, the difference in scores from the hands remains small and, as discussed later, the over-riding consideration for each player is to try to maintain the maximum score in hand.

On the basis of average scores a game should last for nine deals and the winner of the cut would score 120 and the loser 114 points of which 92.5 and 87.5 points respectively come from the hands and the cribs.

Winner of the cut $5 \times (8 + 4.5) + 4 \times 7.5 = 92.5$

Loser of the cut $4 \times (8 + 4.5) + 5 \times 7.5 = 87.5$

For both players the points from the hands and cribs represent about 77% of the total points available and the remaining 23% from the pegging as the cards are played.

$$100 \times \frac{92.5}{120} = 77.08\% \qquad 100 \times \frac{87.5}{114} = 76.75\%$$

On the assumption that the laws of chance apply equally to both players the total points awarded depends on the abilities of the players to make a series of judgements.

(a) To be able to judge which cards should be retained in hand and which should be discarded to the crib, bearing in mind the possible effect of the 'Turn-Up' card on those retained in hand and discarded to the crib, and also bearing in mind the sort of cards likely to be discarded by the opponent. This is a one-off judgement and, once made, cannot be altered. All the cards received by the player are affected by it. The judgement made in selecting the cards to keep in hand can make a major difference to the score obtained. For most of the deals in each game the player will try to hold cards which will give the maximum count. On occasion other tactics should be used when dictated by the position on the board. Details regarding when to change tactics are given later.

(b) To be able to judge the order in which the cards retained in the hand should be played. Here a series of choices has to be made, subsequent ones depending on those already made. At the start it is necessary to choose which of the four cards in hand to play first; this choice affects the further three choices for the second card to play, and so on until there is no choice for the last card.

In order to improve the chance of winning at cribbage it is important never to forget the difference in the points likely to be available to the winner and the loser of the cut. The former should do everything possible to maintain the advantage of having the first deal, the latter trying to overcome this. Here, in particular, both players should remember that, roughly speaking, *one extra point gained can often be worth two, the second being a point that should have been won by the opponent.* Because only eight cards are involved during the play, each card can be considered as contributing one eighth of the total number of points pegged. Each player should, therefore, learn how to play both aggressively and defensively and to change tactics when it is appropriate to do so. Note that although about three times the points are likely to arise from the counts from the hands and the cribs as will be scored by pegging as the cards are played, it does not follow that it is three times as likely that the 'extra' points required to win will be obtained that way. The reverse is more probable, with many of the 'extra' points coming as the cards are played.

Chapter 3

DISCARDING TO THE CRIB

It is the skill of the player in selecting, from the six cards received, which four to retain in hand and which to discard to the crib which has the greatest influence on the chance of winning the game. All the stages of the game are affected by the selection and it is critical that the best should be made. An analysis of the cards played from the ten or so deals that are required to complete each game shows that a mistake in the selection of the hand and the discards for just one of the deals may be the reason for losing the game.

The tactics used by the players when making a selection will often change as the game progresses. In the early stages both players will try to keep cards in their hands which are likely to score by pegging as the cards are played and to score well in combination with the 'Turn-Up' card. In addition the dealer will try to put two cards into the crib which have a reasonable chance of combining with those discarded by the non-dealer and with the 'Turn-Up' card. The non-dealer will try to discard so that the score from the crib is small. This is called 'balking the crib'; cards which are least likely to increase the score from the crib are called good balking cards, and those which are helpful are bad balking cards. All too often a player is not able to make discards which will achieve all of these aims. A choice has to be made based on the risks and benefits involved for each of the possible discards.

In the later stages of the game the non-dealer may be in a position where it is possible to win from the points likely to be gained by pegging together with the score from the cards held in the hand. In such a situation, because the non-dealer is the first to record the points from the hand, it may not be possible for the dealer to score either the points from the hand or those from the crib. Therefore, if the dealer thinks that the deal is likely to be the last of the game and that the non-dealer has a chance of scoring sufficient points to win, the dealer should discard with the aim of getting the maximum number of points from the pegging alone.

Discarding by the dealer

The cards in the hand and crib both score points in combination with the 'Turn-Up' card. On average, because they have been selected as a group, the four cards in the hand score more points than those from the crib and, as a general rule, the dealer should try, when selecting the discards, to aim for the maximum number of points from the hand. However, this rule should not be applied blindly and, for each set of cards, all the possible ways of discarding should be considered. It should always be remembered that each card retained in hand can only give rise to *additional* points in combination with *one* extra card, the 'Turn-Up' card.

It often happens that, regardless of what the 'Turn-Up' card may be, it is unlikely for a reasonable score to be produced from *any* four of the six cards received. It is then wise for the dealer to discard so that there is the best chance of scoring from the crib. Each of the discards has the chance of combining with *three* extra cards, the two discarded by the non-dealer and the 'Turn-Up' card. The probability of gaining *additional* points from the crib is somewhat greater than gaining them from the hand. Putting cards into the crib which have a good chance of scoring points is often called 'salting the crib'. Occasionally the dealer may be able to do this and still maintain a good score in hand.

Sometimes, no matter which two cards are discarded, there is little hope of obtaining a good score from the remaining four. It is then best to keep those offering the greatest chance of scoring as the cards are played. This is also the best approach for the likely last deal of the game if there is little chance of the scores from the hand and crib being recorded.

Discarding by the non-dealer

The non-dealer should try to balk the crib by selecting discards which will be the least likely to offer scoring possibilities. There can frequently be a conflict between the need to keep cards in hand which offer a chance of a good score and, at the same time, being able to put good balking cards into the crib. On such occasions the non-dealer should subtract the likely score that the discards will give to the crib from the likely score from the cards retained in hand. To do this it is necessary to consider the probability of significant scores arising from all four discards with all possible 'Turn-up' cards versus the probability of significant increases in the score from the four cards retained in hand with the same 'Turn-Up' cards. Guidance for judging these probabilities is given later.

Any possible points from the dealer's crib can be disregarded if the non-dealer has a good chance of winning by pegging as the cards are played and from the count in hand. In such cases any of the cards received can be discarded as the points from the crib are not relevant. Furthermore, when the dealer has a chance of winning by pegging as the cards are played, the non-dealer should discard with the aim of getting the maximum points from pegging alone, and if necessary jeopardise the potential score from his hand.

Cards to retain and/or to discard

1. Fives

A 5 will score 15/2 with any of the sixteen '10' cards and, therefore, is a good card for the dealer either to retain in hand or to discard to the crib, whichever is the more appropriate. Although the dealer does not know the values of the non-dealer's discards or that of the 'Turn-Up' card there is always a good chance that at least one of them will be a '10' card. The dealer therefore has a good chance of scoring extra points by discarding a 5 provided the potential score from the hand is maintained. Only under very exceptional circumstances should a 5 be discarded by the non-dealer.

2. Pairs of cards

Pairs of cards are good for either player to retain in hand or for the dealer, but not the non-dealer, to discard to the crib. In the hand there is always the chance of the 'Turn-Up' card increasing the 2 points from the pair to 6 for 'Pairs Royal' or of the pair becoming part of a double sequence. Note that because of the two discards from the non-dealer a pair of cards placed in the crib by the dealer has more chance of increasing the score than when they are kept in the hand. Note also that a pair of cards whose sum is less than 15 is more valuable than a pair with a sum exceeding that. There is always the possibility of the pair of low cards combining with another card to give an extra 15/2.

3. Cards of adjacent rank or separated by one rank

Two cards such as 9 and 10 or 9 and J may become part of sequences. When they are held in the hand they can only rely on the 'Turn-Up' card to complete the sequence. However, when they are discarded to the crib, there is a better chance of the score being increased because of the additional chance of the sequence being completed by one of the opponent's discards. It follows, therefore, that unless there is either some over-riding reason for keeping them in the hand, or there are better discards available, the dealer should discard them. The non-dealer should try to avoid discarding in this way, but it may be unavoidable as the risks of doing so may be less than with other discards.

4. Two cards which add up to 5

Two cards such as (3 + 2) and (4 + A) are good combinations for either player to retain in hand because of the chance of scoring an extra 15/2 if the 'Turn-Up' card is one of the sixteen '10' cards. The (3 + 2) combination is the more desirable as there is the additional chance that they will become part of a sequence if the 'Turn-Up' card is either a 4 or an Ace. The non-dealer should not discard either combination. However, they are excellent cards for the dealer to put in his crib because of the good chance that the non-dealer will have to discard a '10' card. On the other hand, these low cards have a good chance of scoring points by pegging as the cards are played and the dealer should take this into consideration when deciding on the wisdom of discarding either of these combinations.

5. Two card combinations which score 15/2

The non-dealer should never discard the combinations (5 + '10'), (6 + 9) and (7 + 8) unless the points given away for 15/2 and any other points likely to arise via the dealer's discards and the 'Turn-Up' card can be more than recovered by the cards retained in hand.

6. (9 + 7) and (8 + 6) combinations

These are good combinations for either player to retain in hand. There is the possibility of the 'Turn-Up' card scoring an extra 5 points, 2 for 15/2 and 3 for a sequence. It is even better if the dealer is able to discard one of these combinations to the crib because of the additional chance of a fit with one of the discards from the non-dealer. The reverse is true for the non-dealer who should not make such discards unless, because of the state of the game, the dealer is unlikely to be able to record the points from the crib.

7. Two cards of the same suit

A five-card flush in the crib occurs very infrequently. There is therefore little risk that the dealer will score points this way even if the non-dealer discards two cards of the same suit.

8. A Jack

The non-dealer should try not to discard a Jack because of the possibility of giving away 'One for His Nob'.

9. A King

One of the Kings is the least likely of the sixteen '10' cards to score in the crib and is therefore a good discard by the non-dealer. A King can only form a sequence in one direction: the crib must contain a Queen and Jack as well.

10. A King and a 10

If it is necessary for the non-dealer to discard two '10' cards the best combination is (K + 10). This gives the least chance of forming sequences with the dealer's discards and with the 'Turn-Up' card.

Discarding in order to score the maximum by pegging as the cards are played

For most of the deals in a game a player should aim to score the maximum number of points from a combination of the pegging, the hand and, if dealer, from the crib as well. When it is thought that the deal might be the last in a game it is often necessary for one, or both, of the players to ignore all other ways of scoring and to discard with the sole aim of having the best chance of scoring by pegging as the cards are played, even if the potential score from elsewhere is reduced.

Frequently, because the best cards for pegging also score well when retained in hand, there is little controversy in the choice of the discards. However, for the sake of clarity, this section is written with the points pegged as the cards are played as the only consideration, but it should be remembered that it is also relevant to the play of the cards in general.

1. Scoring 15/2

It is probable that at least one of the sixteen '10' cards will be in the opponent's hand and it is therefore wise to keep 5's and (3 + 2) and (4 + A) combinations. Thus, if the opponent leads a '10' card, a 5 will score 15/2 or, if following the lead of a 3, the opponent plays a '10' card , a 2 will also score 15/2. Similarly for the (4 + A) combination.

2. Elevens

It is useful to hold pairs of cards, such as (A + '10'), (2 + 9), (3 + 8), (4 + 7) and (5 + 6), which have a sum adding up to 11. In conjunction with two '10' cards these frequently complete the count to 31 regardless of which player leads first. For example, if following the lead of a 9 from a (2 + 9) combination, cards were played in the order 9, Q, J, 'Go', the first player could then make 31 by playing the 2 from the combination.

3. Pairs

Retain two cards of the same rank. Although 2 points are lost when one of these is led and then paired by the opponent, 6 are gained by playing the other from the pair to score 'Pairs Royal'. Because of the risk of this happening, skilful players will often decline to pair cards in the early stages of play. It can sometimes pay to delay leading from a pair of cards of equal rank until later on when it is not so obvious to the opponent that a pair may be held. Do not keep pairs of cards in hand if the game has reached the stage when it can be decided by pegging alone. It is better to keep four cards of different rank so that there is a greater chance of pairing the opponent's lead.

4. Sequences

Keeping sequences is one of the best ways of obtaining a high count from the hand and, in addition, it is also a good way of gaining points by pegging. For both reasons sequences are likely to be retained in the hand but care needs to be exercised when choosing which card to lead from a sequence. There are no fixed rules for doing this and the choice depends on the cards in the sequence and the position reached in the game. The following suggestions are given as guidance.

(a) Do not lead the Ace when a sequence starts with an Ace. Lead from the centre.

(b) Do not lead the King when the sequence ends with a King. Lead from the centre.

(c) From a double sequence, lead one of the pair of cards of the same rank.

(d) If, after leading a low card which is part of a sequence in hand, the opponent plays a card of adjacent rank or one separated by one rank from that led, be careful before completing the sequence in play. The opponent may well have another card that can also join into the sequence.

Nevertheless, it is safe to complete a three-card sequence in play if it has a cumulative sum of 27, 29 or 30 (i.e., the sequence contains at least one '10' card). No further cards forming part of the sequence can be played because the count would exceed '31'.

(e) Take care when leading from a sequence of three cards of middle rank. For example, if the 7 is led from (6, 7, 8) and the opponent plays an 8 to score 15/2, the temptation of scoring 3 points for a sequence in play, by replying with the 6, should be resisted. The cumulative total would then be 21 and any '10' card would give the opponent 2 points for making 31. However, note the danger if, instead of the 6, the 8 from the sequence was used to score 2 points for a pair. The cumulative total would then be 23 and by playing another 8 the opponent could score 2 points for '31' and a further 6 points for 'Pairs Royal'.

5. Low Cards

Ideally first leads should be ones that give the opponent the least chance of scoring. Aces, 2's, 3's and 4's are all good leads as the opponent cannot score 15/2 from them and the only chance of scoring is by pairing the lead. Furthermore, if after a lead of a 2, 3 or 4 the opponent plays a '10' card , it can safely be paired because a 'Pairs Royal' cannot be made without the total exceeding 31. On the other hand, low cards are also useful for completing the count to 31 and if other leads are available it is sometimes wise not to lead with a low card. Leads from (A + 4) and (2 + 3) combinations are generally worthwhile for the reasons given above.

6. (6 + 9) combinations

If forced to lead from this combination always lead the 6 rather than the 9. Should the opponent play a 9 to score 15/2, the 9 can be paired to give a running total of 24 and a third 9 cannot be played for 'Pairs Royal' without the count exceeding '31'. On the other hand, if the first lead from (6 + 9) had been the 9 and the opponent had then played a 6 for 15/2, the opponent's 6 could not be paired with safety because the cumulative score would then be 21. This would give the opponent the option either of playing any of the '10' cards to score 2 points for reaching 31, or of playing a third 6 to score six points for 'Pairs Royal'.

7. (3 + 9) and (4 + 7) combinations

From these combinations lead the 3 or the 4 so that, if they are paired by the opponent, the 9 or the 7 can be played to score 15/2.

8. Numbers to avoid

Avoid making the sum to <u>*11*</u> by following a 7 with a 4 or the sum to <u>*12*</u> by following a 9 with a 3. Four points are lost if the opponent pairs the 4 or the 3; two points for the pair and two for 15/2. For similar reasons avoid playing a 4 to make the sum <u>*27*</u> and a 3 to make it <u>*28*</u>. Again four points are lost if the opponent pairs the 4 or the 3, two points for the pair and two for '31'. In addition try not to make the sum equal to <u>*21*</u> because it is relatively easy for the opponent to score 2 points by playing one of the '10' cards.

(A more detailed discussion on the best way to obtain the maximum score from pegging as the cards are played is given in Chapter 8.)

Examples showing how to discard to the crib

The examples have been chosen to give the reader practice in discarding to the crib. In the first set of examples the reader should aim to obtain the maximum number of points from the pegging, the hand and the crib.

With the second set of examples the reader is asked to assume that the deal is likely to be the last of the game and to discard accordingly. With all the examples it should be assumed that the same sets of cards have been received by the dealer and the non-dealer and for each the reader is asked to choose the best way of discarding.

The examples are shown in quiz format. The answers to each quiz are given in the Tables in which the cards retained and discarded by the dealer are designated by (a) and those of the non-dealer by (b). The Tables also contain comments by the authors.

Discarding during the main part of the game

Quiz 1

Assume, for each of the following examples, that the same set of cards was received by (a) the dealer and (b) the non-dealer. Which cards should be retained in hand?

The answers to the quiz are given in the authors' comments in the Table below.

1. (A + 7 + 9 + 9 + 10 + J)	**6.** (2 + 2 + 3 + 3 + 3 + K)
2. (2 + 3 + 8 + 10 + 10 + K)	**7.** (A + 4 + 6 + 7 + 8 + 9)
3. (A + 6 + 9 + Q + K + K)	**8.** (2 + 3 + 4 + Q + Q + K)
4. (A + 3 + 7 + 10 + Q + K)	**9.** (6 + 6 + 7 + 8 + 8 + 9)
5. (5 + 6 + 6 + 10 + 10 + 10)	**10.** (4 + 4 + 5 + 5 + 5 + 6)

Answers to Quiz

Example	*Cards received*	*Cards retained*	*Cards discarded*
1	A, 7, 9, 9, 10, J	9, 9, 10, J (a) and (b)	A, 7 (a) and (b)
Comment: Both players should discard in the same way and hold the maximum score in hand.			
2	2, 3, 8, 10, 10, K	2, 3, 10, 10 (a) and (b)	8, K (a) and (b)
Comment: Both players should discard in the same way and hold the maximum score in hand			
3	A, 6, 9, Q, K, K	A, Q, K, K (a) 6, 9, K, K (b)	6, 9 (a) A, Q (b)
Comment: No points are lost if the dealer discards the (6, 9) combination. There is also a better chance of the 'Turn-Up' card increasing the overall score. The non-dealer should hold the maximum score from the hand.			

Example	*Cards received*	*Cards retained*	*Cards discarded*
4	A, 3, 7, 10, Q, K	A, 3, 7, 10 (a)	Q, K (a)
		A, 3, 7, Q (b)	10, K (b)
Comment: No score is possible irrespective of which four cards are retained. There are three sets of cards which have the lowest numerical sum, i.e., (A, 3, 7, 10) or (A, 3, 7, Q) or (A, 3, 7, K). Because the non-dealer is more likely to put a Q or a K into the crib than a 10 the dealer should discard the (Q, K) and hope to score 2 for pair. In addition there is also the possibility of scoring for a sequence if the 'Turn-Up' or one of the opponent's discards is a J. The non-dealer should discard the (10, K) which are the least likely to score in the crib.			
5	5, 6, 6, 10, 10, 10	5,10,10,10 (a) and (b)	6, 6 (a) and (b)
Comment: Both players should discard in the same way. The dealer scores 14 points without any help from the 'Turn-Up' card and from the other discards. The non-dealer should discard in the same way and obtain a guaranteed score of 10 points (12 in hand minus the 2 put into the crib). To discard in any other way would only guarantee a score of 6 points, e.g., (5, 6, 10, 10) retained and (6, 10) discarded, and the 4 points lost cannot be recovered via the 'Turn-Up' card.			
6	2, 2, 3, 3, 3, K	2, 2, 3, K (a)	3, 3 (a)
		2, 3, 3, 3 (b)	2, K (b)
Comment: The dealer should discard in order to achieve the maximum guaranteed score from his hand and crib, i.e., a total of 8 points. The non-dealer should keep the maximum score in hand whilst discarding the worst possible cards to the opponent's crib.			
7	A, 4, 6, 7, 8, 9	6, 7, 8, 9 (a)	A, 4 (a)
		A, 6, 7, 8 (b)	4, 9 (b)
Comment: The dealer should keep the maximum score in hand and put the best possible cards into the crib. Because of the reduced risk of a large score from the dealer's crib the non-dealer should discard (4, 9) rather than (A, 4), even though one less point is scored from the cards retained in hand.			
8	2, 3, 4, Q, Q, K	2, 3, 4, K (a)	Q, Q (a)
		2, 3, Q, Q (b)	4, K (b)
Comment: The dealer should discard to get the maximum guaranteed score of 7 points from the hand and crib (i.e., 5 points from the hand and 2 from the crib). The non-dealer should keep the maximum score of 6 points from the hand whilst discarding poor cards to the opponent's crib.			
9	6, 6, 7, 8, 8, 9	6, 7, 8, 8 (a) and (b)	6, 9 (a) and (b)
Comment: Both players should discard in the same way. The dealer gets a guaranteed 14 points (i.e., 12 from the hand plus 2 from the crib) and the non-dealer 10 points (12 from the hand minus 2 from the crib). Fewer points are obtained if the non-dealer chooses any of the other possible hands and the discards are likely to be even more beneficial to the opponent's crib (e.g., 6, 7, 8, 9 retained and 6, 8 discarded).			

Example	*Cards received*	*Cards retained*		*Cards discarded*	
10	4, 4, 5, 5, 5, 6	4, 4, 5, 6	(a)	5, 5	(a)
		4, 5, 5, 6	(b)	4, 5	(b)

Comment: The dealer should discard two 5's and expect the 'Turn-Up' card and the opponent's discards to increase the overall score beyond the 12 points from the hand and the 2 points from the crib. The non-dealer should also hold the maximum score of 12 points from the hand but, to do so, has to discard one of the 5's. However, because 8 is the maximum number of points that can be scored from the hand if no 5's are discarded (e.g., 4, 5, 5, 5 retained and 4, 6 discarded), the non-dealer would be unlucky if holding the maximum resulted in the loss of 4 or more points.

Discarding when it is thought that the deal will be the last of the game

In these examples it is assumed that the score from the crib will not be recorded and that both players will discard hoping to score well by pegging as the cards are played and from the count in hand. In addition, because the non-dealer is always the first to record the points from the hand, there are some occasions when the dealer should discard with the points from the pegging as the only consideration.

Quiz 2

Assume, for each of the following examples, that the same set of cards was received by (a) the dealer and (b) the non-dealer. Which cards should be retained in hand?

The answers to the quiz are given in the authors' comments in the Table below.

11. (2 + 3 + 9 + J + Q + K)

12. (2 + 4 + 5 + 8 + 10 + Q)

13. (A + A + 2 + Q + Q + K)

14. (6 +6 + 7 + 7 + 8 + 9)

15. (2 + 3 + 4 + 5 + 6 + 7)

Answers to Quiz

Example	*Cards received*	*Cards retained*	*Cards discarded*
11	2, 3, 9, J, Q, K	2, 3, 9, J (a)	Q, K (a)
		2, 3, J, Q (b)	9, K (b)
Comment: If points from pegging are the only consideration the dealer may feel it is better to keep (2, 3, 9, J) rather than (2, 3, J, Q), although the former scores 2 points less. The non-dealer is the first to record the points from the hand and should keep the maximum score possible unless the dealer has a good chance of winning by pegging alone.			
12	2, 4, 5, 8, 10, Q	2, 4, 5, 8 (a) and (b)	10, Q (a) and (b)
Comment: There is a better chance of pegging from the (2, 4, 5, 8) than from (4, 5, 10, Q) but at the expense of a smaller score from the hand.			
13	A, A, 2, Q, Q, K	A, A, 2, Q (a) and (b)	Q, K (a) and (b)
Comment: The combination (A, A, 2, Q) affords the most chances of scoring by pegging. However, if the only hope of winning is by getting a large score as the cards are played, it is better to hold (A, A, Q, Q) and gamble on scoring at least one 'Pairs Royal'.			
14	6, 6, 7, 7, 8, 9	6, 7, 8, 9 (a) and (b)	6, 7 (a) and (b)
Comment: If the game can be won without using the maximum score from the hand it is better for either of the players to hold four different cards in sequence, (6, 7, 8, 9), than to hold a double sequence, (6, 7, 7, 8). The former gives the greater chance of scoring, either from 15/2, or by pairing the lead or by forming part of a running sequence.			
15	2, 3, 4, 5, 6, 7	2, 3, 4, 5 (a) and (b)	6, 7 (a) and (b)
Comment: If no score from the hand is required it is best to retain (2, 3, 4, 5). If points from the hand are required then, because it is the general view that low cards are the most likely to score when pegging, most players would choose to hold (3, 4, 5, 6) rather than (4, 5, 6, 7), both of which score 6 points.			

Chapter 4

THREE-HANDED CRIBBAGE

The rules are the same as those for two-handed six-card cribbage and each game consists of 121 points. The three players cut the cards to decide who shall deal first, lowest winning and Ace counting low. If the lowest card is cut by two players then all three must cut again. The deal rotates clockwise and continues to rotate into the next and subsequent games.

The cards are dealt clockwise, one at a time, until each player has five cards. One further card, forming part of the crib, is dealt face down in front of the dealer. The crib is completed by each player discarding one card so that the crib and each hand all contain four cards.

The cards are played and scored in the same way as in the two-handed six-card game. However, when a player cannot play a card without the sum exceeding 31 and calls 'Go', the next player must play a card if he is able to do so.

Play continues until none of the players can play. The sum is then started again by the player immediately to the left of the last to play and this process continues until all the cards in the three hands have been played.

A player who has said 'Go', but could have played, forfeits 2 points to each of the other two players. The hands and crib are scored in the usual way, starting with the player to the left of the dealer, and with the dealer being the last to record the points from his hand and crib.

Strategy and tactics

These are very similar to those suggested for the two-handed game, but there are a few differences which are worth mentioning.

1. Each player has two opponents instead of one. The leader at each stage of the game can therefore expect both opponents to combine their efforts to reduce the lead even if it means one of them improving his position relative to the other. For example, when a low card is led so that it is possible for a sequence of cards to be formed before 'Go', the second player should be particularly careful not to play a card with a rank close to that which was led. Otherwise the third player may be able to complete a sequence of three cards and the first player, when his turn comes again, may be able either to make the sequence up to four cards or to complete another three card sequence.

2. Because each player discards only one card the dealer has less opportunity of 'salting' his crib than is possible in the two-handed game. In addition whereas in the two-handed game the score in the crib is only affected by one 'wild' card, i.e., the 'Turn-Up' card, in the three-handed game there are two 'wild' cards, the 'Turn-Up' and the card dealt into the crib. The score from the crib therefore tends to be more variable than in the two-handed game and less reliance should be placed on it when assessing the tactics to be used at each stage of the game.

3. Because there are three players, and because it is more difficult to predict the number of deals required to complete a game, there is less opportunity of influencing the outcome by changes in tactics. Although it is an interesting game to play there is a much greater element of chance involved.

TWO AGAINST ONE

This is a variation of the three-handed game in which two of the players compete against the third. The partnership is required to score 121 points and the single player 61 to win the game. The usual rules for cribbage apply.

Strategy and tactics

The partnership has the better chance of winning as there are several ways in which the partners can co-operate to score points. It is therefore only fair that the games are played in groups of three with each player taking it in turn to play against the other two.

1. Both players in the partnership should always try to put a good card into their own and their partner's crib. Of course, table talk is not allowed and the partners cannot discuss which cards they are retaining or putting into the crib.

The score from their crib is therefore likely to be increased relative to that of the single player and, because between them they will score from about six cribs in each game, this will have a major impact on the outcome of the game.

2. It is often difficult for the lone player to find a lead which will stop the partnership from scoring. A '10' card is generally the safest lead, especially if an Ace is held as well. A lead of a 7 or 8 should be avoided.

3. The partnership should be able to peg more points as the cards are played than when they play as individuals. For example, with the partners playing consecutively, a lead of a 5 by the first gives a good chance of a score of 15/2 by the second in the partnership. Furthermore the partnership can capitalize on the order of play to score highly.

For the purpose of illustration let the two players in the partnership be A and B and the lone player be C and let the order of play be BCABCA etc. The examples in the Table below show the danger to the player C when scoring after B has led a 7 (individual scores are shown in brackets). Only some of the many possibilities, all with sums adding up to 31, are shown in the Table.

Players A and B versus Player C

B	C	A	B	C	Points for A + B	Points for C
7	8 (2)	9 (3)	7 (5)		8	2
7	8 (2)	8 (2)	8 (8)		10	2
7	8 (2)	6 (3)	9 (4)	A (2)	7	4
7	8 (2)	6 (3)	7 (3)	3 (2)	6	4
7	7 (2)	7 (6)	Q (2)		8	2
7	7 (2)	8	9 (5)		5	2

Bearing in mind that the partnership has to score twice as many points as the lone player, the examples in the Table show that if the lone player scores 2 points when replying to a lead of a 7 there is a good chance that the partnership will peg more than twice as many points during that particular count to '31' or 'Go'.

Similar problems occur if the lone player scores 2 points after a lead of an 8, 6 or 9 and in each case the opponents' replies may score heavily. It is generally wise for the lone player to follow the opening lead by 'playing away' using a card that is at least three ranks different from the lead.

Chapter 5

FOUR-HANDED CRIBBAGE

The game is played by two pairs of partners with the players in each partnership sitting opposite to each other. The rules are the same as those for the two-handed six-card game. All four of the players cut for the first deal, Ace counting low and the lowest winning. The deal then rotates in a clockwise direction and a game consists of 121 points. One of the players from each side is chosen to score all the points from the partnership; the partner is not allowed to touch the pegs on the cribbage board, but is allowed to advise about any errors and omissions which are observed.

The pack is then cut by the player to the right of the dealer who then deals the cards, one at a time, in a clockwise direction and starting with the player to his left, until each player has five cards. Each player discards one card so that the crib and the hands each contain four cards. The player to the left of the dealer cuts the remainder of the pack and the dealer exposes the 'Turn-Up' card. The cards are then played in the same way as in three-handed cribbage with the player to the left of the dealer making the first lead.

When a player calls 'Go' because he is unable to play without the sum exceeding 31, the player to his left must play if he can, and so on until none of the players has a card which can be played. A new sum is then started by the player to the left of the last one playing in the previous sum and play continues until all sixteen cards from the hands have been used. After the cards have been played the counts from the hands are recorded clockwise in order, the dealer being the last to score. The crib is recorded last of all.

Strategy and tactics

Every opportunity should be taken to get the maximum number of points from the partnership. Cards which are likely to increase the score should be discarded to one's own and partner's crib unless, towards the final stages of a game, it may not be possible to record the score from the crib. The reverse is true when discarding to the opponent's crib, with face cards, and particularly Kings, being the least likely to so.

The lead is often critical to the number of points scored by pegging and, unless they are unavoidable, some leads are unwise. The cards played following the lead can also have a major effect on the number of points scored. For the purpose of illustration let the partnerships be (A + C) and (B + D), let A be the leader of the first card in each sum and let the order of play be ABCD. For all of the examples listed in the Table overleaf, the total numerical sum is 31. The points scored during play are shown in brackets. For some of the examples the order of the cards played is highly probable; for others not so.

<table>
<tr><th>Example</th><th>A</th><th>B</th><th>C</th><th>D</th><th>A</th><th>B</th><th>Total for (A + C)</th><th>Total for (B + D)</th></tr>
<tr><td>1</td><td>5</td><td>Q (2)</td><td>K</td><td>6 (2)</td><td></td><td></td><td>0</td><td>4</td></tr>
<tr><td colspan="9">Comment: Do not lead a 5. There are sixteen ‘10’ cards in the pack and it is quite probable that the next player will have one and can score 15/2.</td></tr>
<tr><td>2</td><td>9</td><td>6 (2)</td><td>6 (2)</td><td>K (2)</td><td></td><td></td><td>2</td><td>4</td></tr>
<tr><td>3</td><td>6</td><td>9 (2)</td><td>9 (2)</td><td>7 (2)</td><td></td><td></td><td>2</td><td>4</td></tr>
<tr><td colspan="9">Comment: When choosing between a lead of either a 9 or a 6, always choose the 6. If following a lead of a 9, the second player makes 15/2 by playing a 6, the third player cannot score 2 by the 6 without making a running total of 21, which leaves the fourth player able to score 2 points for ‘31’ by playing one of the sixteen ‘10’ cards. On the other hand with a sequence of three cards 6 + 9 + 9 the running total is 24 and there are only four 7’s in the pack with which to make ‘31’.</td></tr>
<tr><td>4</td><td>7</td><td>8 (2)</td><td>8 (2)</td><td>8 (8)</td><td></td><td></td><td>2</td><td>10</td></tr>
<tr><td>5</td><td>7</td><td>8 (2)</td><td>6 (3)</td><td>Q (2)</td><td></td><td></td><td>3</td><td>4</td></tr>
<tr><td>6</td><td>7</td><td>8 (2)</td><td>6 (3)</td><td>9 (4)</td><td>A (2)</td><td></td><td>5</td><td>6</td></tr>
<tr><td>7</td><td>7</td><td>7 (2)</td><td>7 (6)</td><td>K (2)</td><td></td><td></td><td>6</td><td>4</td></tr>
<tr><td colspan="9">Comment: These four examples all involve a lead of a 7. With such a lead it is likely that points will be scored by one or both members of the partnerships. It is a lead to avoid if it is thought that, in the final stages of the game, the opposition can win with the score from pegging alone. On the other hand a lead of a 7 if the partnership is well ahead or is so close to scoring 121 that the gamble of pegging out before the opposition should be taken. Similar remarks apply for a lead of an 8.</td></tr>
<tr><td>8</td><td>4</td><td>6</td><td>5 (5)</td><td>4 (3)</td><td>6 (3)</td><td>6 (4)</td><td>8</td><td>7</td></tr>
<tr><td>9</td><td>3</td><td>6</td><td>6 (4)</td><td>8</td><td>8 (4)</td><td></td><td>0</td><td>8</td></tr>
<tr><td>10</td><td>2</td><td>J</td><td>3 (2)</td><td>3 (2)</td><td>3 (6)</td><td>Q (2)</td><td>8</td><td>4</td></tr>
<tr><td colspan="9">Comment: These three examples all involve the lead of a low card. Following such a lead the second player can only score by pairing it and, if unable to do so, may well have to play a card of close rank or a ‘10’ card. The third player then has a good chance of scoring either by making 15/2 or by completing a sequence or by pairing the second player’s reply. In addition, a lead of a low card can give rise to a significant score if the players in the partnership have previously agreed that, when the position in the game is appropriate, both of them will keep low cards in hand. For example, with player A as the dealer in what is likely to be the final deal of the game the players know that, because of the order in which the points from the hands and the crib are recorded on the board, those from A’s hand and crib are unlikely to count. By both of them keeping low cards in their hands they have more opportunity to gain points by pegging.</td></tr>
</table>

Chapter 6

MAXIMISING THE SCORE

Chance governs both the values of the cards dealt to each player and that of the 'Turn-Up' card. It is impossible to score well with a set of poor cards but, in the long run, chance ensures that each player will receive cards of similar quality. That being so, when selecting which cards to retain in hand and which to discard to the crib, it is helpful if a player can develop a feeling for the cards which cannot be seen.

On picking up the cards a player knows only the values of those received, and for two-handed six-card cribbage, can only guess at the way in which the remaining 46 cards are distributed between those dealt to the opponent and those that remain in the pack. Even so it is of great help when discarding to the crib to be able to judge which four of the six cards are most likely to be benefited by the 'Turn-Up' card. In addition, both before and as the cards are played, it is useful if educated guesses can be made of the remaining cards in the opponent's hand.

A detailed mathematical approach to the game of cribbage is not necessary and, in many ways, would be unwise. It is important, as explained elsewhere, to vary the tactics used at different stages of the game and this cannot be done when using a rigid approach based on mathematical probabilities. To get the maximum score from each deal a player should use all the available options, one being the ability to make rapid assessments of which cards are most likely to be involved in the scoring.

There are 4 cards of each rank in a full pack of 52 cards and, therefore, for a fully shuffled pack placed face down, there is a 1/52 or 1/13 chance that the top card will be of a specified rank. Similarly, because there are sixteen '10' cards in a full pack, there is a 16/52 or 4/13 chance, or (1 in 3.25) chance, of the top card being one of them.

If some of the cards are removed from the pack the chance that a card of specified rank will be the top card of the stockpile is changed and depends on the number of cards removed and on their ranks. Thus if six cards are removed, and three of them are '10' cards, the cards remaining in the stockpile will contain thirteen '10' cards and there will be a 13/46 chance, or (1 in 3.54) chance, of the top card of the stockpile being a '10' card. It would be pointless, and there would be no time, during a game of cards to stop and calculate chances associated with all the variations of play that are likely to occur.

Neither player can calculate the likelihood of a particular card being discarded to the crib by the opponent, this depending on the cards dealt, the state of the game and the skill of the opponent. However, certain cards are less likely to be discarded than others and the skilful player will take this into account.

Despite the difficulties it is important that a player should have the ability to scan each set of six cards received and to judge the chances of any four of them scoring *extra* points when combined with the 'Turn-Up' card. It is also important to be able to judge the chances of the 'Turn-Up' card combining with those discarded to the crib. By doing this a player should be able to gain the maximum number of points from each deal.

Increase in the score from the hand due to the 'Turn-Up' Card

The six cards a player receives enables him to judge the likelihood of the 'Turn-Up' card increasing the score for those retained in hand and, to a lesser extent, for those discarded to the crib. From the point of view of calculating the possible effect of the 'Turn-Up' card on the cards retained in hand it can be assumed that the opponent does not exist and that all of the 46 unknown cards are in the stockpile.

For the purpose of illustrating this a random set of cards has been used in Table 6.1.

Table 6.1

Cards received	Cards retained	Rank of 'Turn-Up'	Number available	Increase in score
3, 4, 6, 9, 10, K	3, 4, 6, 9	A	4	0
		2	4	7
		3	3	4
		4	3	2
		5	4	6
		6	3	6
		7	4	0
		8	4	2
		9	3	4
		10	3	0
		J	4	0
		Q	4	0
		K	3	0

For the particular set of six cards shown in Table 6.1, not all the 46 'unknown' cards can give an increase in the score for the four selected as the hand. There is no increase if the 'Turn-Up' card is an A, 7,10, J, Q or K. Cards of the other ranks all increase the score, but by differing amounts, and the chance of their being the 'Turn-Up' card is not necessarily the same. For example, the player knows, because of the values of the cards dealt to him, that amongst the 46 unknown cards there are four 2's but only three 3's.

The total number of cards which can give an increase in the score is the sum of all the 2's, 3's, 4's, 5's, 6's, 8's and 9's in the 46 cards, i.e., 4 + 3 + 3 + 4 + 3 + 4 + 3 = 24 cards. The weighted average increase in the score for the four cards retained in hand can also be calculated. There are four 2's each giving an increase of 7, three 3's each giving an increase of 4, and so on, for all of the cards which can give an increase. The total increase in the score for all of the cards which can give part of that total is, therefore:

$$4 \times 7 + 3 \times 4 + 3 \times 2 + 4 \times 6 + 3 \times 6 + 4 \times 2 + 3 \times 4 = 108.$$

The total increase in the score arises from the individual scores of the 46 possible 'Turn-Up' cards and, therefore, the weighted average increase in the score = 108/46 or 2.35 points.

There are fifteen different ways of selecting four cards from the six received from the dealer. It would be neither sensible nor practical, for every combination of four, to calculate the weighted average increase in the score, and the likelihood of getting it, for all of the possible 'Turn-Up' cards associated with that deal. *However it is possible to scan the cards and to select those four which are most likely to combine with the 'Turn-Up' card and, by making the correct selection, obtain extra points from the hands and increase the chance of winning the game.* The examples in the Quizzes and Tables below have been chosen to illustrate how to make the selection rapidly and accurately. Only some of the ways of selecting four cards from six are shown in the examples, with the scores from those retained being shown in parentheses. *It should be noted that the values for the weighted average increase in the scores, and the probability of obtaining them, are only given for the purpose of illustrating the procedure to be followed when making the selection.*

No allowances have been made in this section for any extra points which might be scored for 'One for his Nob' and for flushes. However, the four, and possibly five, points which can be gained for a flush are not insignificant. When there are four cards of the same suit amongst the six received from the dealer it is necessary for the player to make a separate judgement regarding the wisdom, or not, of keeping the flush. This aspect of selecting the hand is dealt with separately and illustrative examples are shown in Table 6.8

The odds that 'One for His Nob' will be scored depends on how many Jacks have been dealt to the two players and it is unusual for this to have an influence on the selection of the cards to be retained. If the non-dealer receives two Jacks and decides to discard one of them, the Jack chosen should be, if possible, the one which is of the same suit as one or more of the other cards received. By doing this, the dealer has a slightly smaller chance of scoring 'One for His Nob'.

If the advice given below is followed, the hand selected will have the maximum chance of the best increase in the score from the 'Turn-Up' card. It must be emphasised that the selection procedure only examines the effect of the 'Turn-Up' card on the four cards retained in hand and the two discarded to the crib. Both players should always make allowance for the effect that the other discards have on the potential score in the crib. Such aspects are considered in the comments made in the Tables.

Selection Procedure

Deals for which only one selection gives the maximum score for the hand

Advice to the dealer

Keep the selection giving the maximum score unless there is another selection, differing by only 2 points from the one with the maximum score, which allows a 5 *or a* (2 + 3) *combination or an* (A + 4) *combination to be discarded to the crib. If so that selection should be retained.*

Advice to the non-dealer

Keep the selection giving the maximum score unless, by doing so, it is necessary to discard either a 5 *or a* (2 + 3) *or a* (A + 4) *and the difference in the scores from the selection retained and from that with the maximum score is two or less. If the difference in the scores from the selections is greater than two, discard the* 5 *or the* (2 + 3) or the (A + 4) *combination as it is unlikely that any extra score from the crib will be as great as that lost by not keeping the maximum score.*

Quiz

Assume, for each of the following examples, that the same sets of cards were received by (a) the dealer and (b) the non-dealer.

Which cards should be retained in hand?

The answers to the quiz are given in the authors' comments in Table 6.2.

1. (6 + 7 + 8 + 9 + J + K)	**4.** (2 + 3 + 6 + 7 + J + K)
2. (2 + 2 + 3 + 5 + 7 + 8)	**5.** (A + 5 + 6 + 7 + 8 + 8)
3. (A + 4 + 6 + 7 + 10 + Q)	**6.** (2 + 3 + 6 + 6 + 8 + 9)

Answers to quiz

Table 6.2					
Only one selection with the maximum score					
Effect of Turn-Up card on score from cards retained and discarded					
Example	Cards Received	Selection for Hand and Discards	Numerical Sum of Selection for Hand	Number of Scoring Turn-Up Cards	Weighted Average Increase in Score
1A	6, 7, 8, 9, J, K	6, 7, 8, 9 (8)	30	28	2.61
		J, K (0)		14	0.87
1B	6, 7,. 8, 9, J, K	6, 7, 8, K (5)	31	28	2.24
		9, J (0)		17	0.83
Comment: Both players should keep selection 1A.					
2A	2, 2, 3, 5, 7, 8	2, 2, 5, 8 (6)	17	34	2.17
		3, 7 (0)		12	0.52
2B	2, 2, 3, 5, 7, 8	2, 5, 7, 8 (4)	22	42	2.87
		2, 3 (0)		29	1.43
Comment: The dealer should keep selection 2A. However, if well behind on the cribbage board, it is worth taking the gamble that the opponent will discard two '10' cards: keep selection 2B and discard the (2 + 3) combination. The non-dealer should keep selection 2A.					
3A	A, 4, 6, 7, 10, Q	A, 4, 10, Q (4)	25	24	2.26
		6, 7 (0)		22	1.30
3B	A, 4, 6, 7, 10, Q	A, 4, 6, 10 (2)	21	35	2.48
		7, Q (0)		14	0.61
Comment: Both players should keep selection 3A.					
4A	2, 3, 6, 7, J, K	2, 3, J, K (4)	25	32	2.78
		6, 7 (0)		21	1.28
4B	2, 3, 6, 7, J, K	2, 3, 7, J (2)	22	42	2.70
		6, K (0)		14	0.61
Comment: Both players should keep selection 4A.					

5A	A, 5, 6, 7, 8, 8	6, 7, 8, 8 (12)	29	22	2.61
		A, 5 (0)		26	1.13
5B	A, 5, 6, 7, 8, 8	5, 6, 7, 8 (6)	26	46	3.52
		A, 8 (0)		11	0.48
Comment: The dealer should keep selection 5A. The non-dealer should also keep selection 5A although this means discarding a 5. The dealer is very unlikely to score, from the crib, the 6 points which would be lost from the hand if selection 5B was chosen.					
6A	2, 3, 6, 6, 8, 9	6, 6, 8, 9 (6)	29	23	2.39
		2, 3 (0)		30	1.48
6B	2, 3, 6, 6, 8, 9	2, 3, 6, 6 (4)	17	39	3.09
		8, 9 (0)		16	1.04
Comment: The dealer should keep selection 6A. The non-dealer should keep selection 6B although, relative to selection 6A, two points are lost by doing so. There is a good chance that these points will be recovered if the 'Turn-Up' card is a '10' card. In addition if selection 6A is chosen there is an even greater chance of losing points because of the additional possibility of the dealer's discards containing at least one '10' card.					

Deals for which more than one selection give the maximum score for the hand

Advice to the dealer

Keep the selection for which the four cards have the smallest numerical sum unless there is another selection, also giving the maximum score without the help of the 'Turn-Up' card, which would provide two discards with a much better chance of scoring points from the crib. Do not keep four cards in hand which score less than the maximum possible in the hope that extra points from the 'Turn-Up' card and the crib will more than compensate for the deficit.

Advice to the non-dealer

Keep the selection for which the four cards have the smallest numerical sum unless there is another selection, also giving the maximum score without the help of the 'Turn-Up' card, which would provide two discards which give less chance of points being scored from the crib.

If, by keeping a selection with the maximum score, it is necessary to discard either a 5 or a (2 + 3) or an (A + 4) and the maximum score is only two points greater than from another selection, choose this other selection, BUT if the maximum scoring selection is more than two points greater than from any other selection, discard the 5 or the (2 + 3) or the (A + 4) combination, as it is unlikely that any extra score from the crib will be as great as those lost by not keeping the maximum score.

Quizzes

Assume, for each of the following examples, that the same sets of cards were received by (a) the dealer and (b) the non-dealer. Which cards should be retained in hand?

For the sake of clarity the examples in this section have been divided into four groups ranging from those giving a low score (which may be zero) to those giving high scoring hands. A fifth group dealing with unusual hands is also included.

The answers to each quiz, together with the authors' comments, are given in the Table which follows it.

Quiz on low scoring hands

7. (2 + 4 + 6 + 8 + 10 + Q)	**9.** (A + 3 + 4 + 6 + 8 + 10)
8. (4 + 6 + 8 + 10 + J + K)	**10.** (A + 2 + 4 + 6 + 7 + Q)

Answers to quiz

Table 6.3 (low scoring hands)

More than one selection giving the maximum score

Effect of 'Turn-Up' card on score from cards retained and discarded

Example	Cards Received	Selection for Hand and Discards	Numerical Sum of Selection for Hand	Number of Scoring 'Turn-Up' Cards	Weighted Average Increase in Score
7A	2, 4, 6, 8, 10, Q	2, 4, 6, 8 (0)	20	32	3.04
		10, Q (0)		14	0.87
7B	2, 4, 6, 8, 10, Q	6, 8, 10, Q (0)	34	32	2.17
		2, 4 (0)		14	0.69
7C	2, 4, 6, 8, 10, Q	2, 4, 10, Q (0)	26	32	2.26
		6, 8 (0)		18	1.04
7D	2, 4, 6, 8, 10, Q	2, 6, 10, Q (0)	28	32	1.83
		4, 8 (0)		14	0.61

Comment: No score is possible for any selection of four cards from the six received. Hands of this type are sometimes called 'bust hands' and they occur with a frequency of about one in ten. Note that the 'Turn-Up' card gives the greatest weighted average increase in the score when the numerical sum of the cards in hand is as small as possible. Both players should keep selection 7A.

8A	4, 6, 8, 10, J, K	4, 6, 8, 10 (0)	28	32	2.52
		J, K (0)		14	0.87
8B	4, 6, 8, 10, J, K	4, 6, 10, J (0)	30	28	2.35
		8, K (0)		14	0.61
8C	4, 6, 8, 10, J, K	6, 8, 10, J (0)	34	32	2.26
		4, K (0)		14	0.61
8D	4, 6, 8, 10, J, K	8, 10, J, K (0)	38	28	1.91
		4, 6 (0)		14	0.87

Comment: No score is possible for any selection. The dealer should keep selection 8A. The non-dealer should choose selection 8B, although it has a slightly smaller chance of forming a sequence with the 'Turn-Up' card, because the discards are less likely to score points in the crib.

9A	A, 3, 4, 6, 8, 10	A, 3, 4, 10 (2)	18	39	2.83
		6, 8 (0)		17	1.00
9B	A, 3, 4, 6, 8, 10	3, 4, 6, 8 (2)	21	31	2.74
		A, 10 (0)		13	0.57
9C	A, 3, 4, 6, 8, 10	A, 4, 8, 10 (2)	23	46	2.48
		3, 6 (0)		10	0.57

Comment: The dealer should keep selection 9A.
The non-dealer should keep either selection 9B or 9C (preferably the former) which, although not having the lowest numerical sum, avoids having to discard (6, 8) to the crib. As general rule the benefit of the 'Turn-Up' card decreases with an increase in the numerical sum of the cards retained.

10A	A, 2, 4, 6, 7, Q	2, 4, 6, 7 (2)	19	28	2.91
		A, Q (0)		13	0.57
10B	A, 2, 4, 6, 7, Q	A, 2, 4, Q (2)	17	40	2.61
		6, 7 (0)		21	1.26
10C	A, 2, 4, 6, 7, Q	2, 6, 7, Q (2)	25	28	2.13
		A, 4 (0)		21	0.91

Comment: The dealer should keep selection 10C and discard the (A + 4) combination to the crib because there is a good chance that the 'Turn-Up' card and/or at least one of the opponent's discards will be a '10' card.
The non-dealer should keep selection 10A, even though it hasn't the lowest numerical sum, and put the best balking cards to the crib whilst maintaining the maximum score from the cards retained.

Quiz on moderate scoring hands

11. (2 + 2 + 4 + 4 + 6 + 6)	**13.** (2 + 3 + 10 + J + Q + K)
12. (8 + 9 + 10 + J + Q + K)	

Answers to quiz

Table 6.4 (moderate scoring hands)

More than one selection giving the maximum score

Effect of 'Turn-Up' card on score from cards retained and discarded

Example	Cards Received	Selection for Hand and Discards	Numerical Sum of Selection for Hand	Number of Scoring 'Turn-Up' Cards	Weighted Average Increase in Score
11A	2, 2, 4, 4, 6, 6	2, 2, 4, 4 (4)	12	20	3.13
		6, 6 (2)		10	0.70
11B	2, 2, 4, 4, 6, 6	4, 4, 6, 6 (4)	20	24	3.13
		2. 2 (2)		2	0.17
11C	2, 2, 4, 4, 6, 6	2, 2, 6, 6 (4)	16	24	2.26
		4, 4 (2)		6	0.35
11D	2, 2, 4, 4, 6, 6	2, 4, 4, 6 (2)	16	26	3.30
		2, 6 (0)		12	0.52

Comment: The dealer should keep selection 11A with a guaranteed score of 6 points from the hand and crib.
The non-dealer scores only 2 points from any of the selections shown because, although with the first three 4 points are scored from the hand, 2 points are also donated to the crib. The non-dealer should therefore keep selection 11D which gives the best chance of forming a sequence with the 'Turn-Up' card as well as giving the best balking cards.

12A	8, 9,10,J,Q,K	8, 9, 10, J (4)	37	27	2.41
		Q, K (0)		13	0.80
12B	8, 9,10,J,Q,K	9, 10, J, Q (4)	39	26	2.39
		8, K (0)		14	0.61
12C	8, 9,10,J,Q,K	10, J, Q, K (4)	40	19	2.33
		8, 9 (0)		17	1.07

Comment: The dealer should choose either selection 12A or 12C. The latter gives the more promising discards whilst the former gives more chance of scoring by pegging. The choice rests on the position held relative to that of the opponent and on whether the deal is likely to be the last of the game.
The non-dealer should keep selection 12B and discard the best balking cards.

13A	2, 3, 10, J, Q, K	2, 3, 10, J (4)	25	34	2.89
		Q, K (0)		13	0.80
13B	2, 3, 10, J, Q, K	2, 3, Q, K (4)	25	30	2.63
		10, J (0)		17	1.07
13C	2, 3, 10, J, Q, K	10, J, Q, K (4)	40	20	2.35
		2, 3 (0)		26	1.30

Comment: For most deals in a game the dealer should keep selection 13C because, although relative to selection 13A the potential score from the hand is reduced, the (2 + 3) combination discarded is likely to enhance the score from the crib. For the final deal in a game the dealer should keep selection 13A because of its better pegging potential. The non-dealer should keep selection 13A.

Quiz on average scoring hands

14. (4 + 5 + 6 + 9 + 10 + Q)	**16.** (2 + 3 + 4 + 5 + 6 + 7)
15. (A + 3 + 4 + 5 + 6 + 7)	**17.** (8 + 9 + 10 + 10 + J + Q)

Answers to quiz

Table 6.5 (average scoring hands)

More than one selection with the maximum score

Effect of 'Turn-Up' card on score from cards retained and discarded

Example	Cards Received	Selection for Hand and Discards	Numerical Sum of Selection for Hand	Number of Scoring 'Turn-Up' Cards	Weighted Average Increase in Score
14A	4, 5, 6, 9,10, Q	4, 5, 6, 9 (7)	24	42	2.89
		10, Q (0)		13	0.78
14B	4, 5, 6, 9,10. Q	4, 5, 6,10 (7)	25	38	2.72
		9, Q (0)		12	0.52
14C	4, 5, 6, 9,10, Q	4, 5, 6, Q (7)	25	38	2.72
		9, 10 (0)		20	1.04

Comment: There are three possible selections which give the maximum score. The dealer should choose selection 14A with the lowest numerical sum.
The non-dealer should choose selection 14B because the discards have the least chance of scoring in the crib.

15A	A, 3, 4, 5, 6, 7	3, 4, 5, 6 (6)	18	46	3.85
		A, 7 (0)		10	0.57
15B	A, 3, 4, 5, 6, 7	4, 5, 6, 7 (6)	22	43	3.59
		A, 3 (0)		10	0.52
Comment: Both players should keep selection 15A, which has the lowest numerical sum.					
16A	2, 3, 4, 5, 6, 7	3, 4, 5, 6 (6)	18	46	3.83
		2, 7 (0)		13	0.57
16B	2, 3, 4, 5, 6, 7	4, 5, 6, 7 (6)	22	42	3.54
		2, 3 (0)		29	1.41
Comment: The dealer should keep selection 16B and hope to obtain a good score from the crib because of the (2 + 3) combination discarded. The non-dealer should keep selection 16A.					
17A	8, 9, 10, 10, J, Q	8, 9, 10, 10 (8)	37	23	2.35
		J, Q (0)		16	1.00
17B	8, 9, 10,10, J, Q	9, 10, 10, J (8)	39	22	2.30
		8, Q (0)		14	0.61
17C	8, 9, 10, 10, J, Q	10, 10, J, Q (8)	40	19	2.35
		8, 9 (0)		16	1.00
Comment: The dealer should keep selection 17A rather than 17C because the opponent is more likely to discard a '10' card. In addition selection 17A offers the better chance of scoring points by pegging. The non-dealer should keep selection 17B which gives the best balking cards to the crib.					

Quiz on high scoring hands

18 (6 + 6 + 7 + 7 + 8 + 8)	**20.** (4 + 4 + 5 + 6 + 6 + K)
19. (7 + 7 + 8 + 8 + 9 + 9)	

Answers to quiz

With hands such as these there is always the chance, though a small one, of the 'Turn-Up' card providing a very large increase to the score. For example, with selection 18A the score is doubled to 24 if the 'Turn-Up' card is an 8. However, because there are only two 8's remaining among the possible 'Turn-Up' cards the chance of obtaining that increase is very low.

Table 6.6 (high scoring hands)

More than one selection with the maximum score

Effect of 'Turn-Up' card on score from cards retained and discarded

Example	Cards Received	Selection for Hand and Discards	Numerical Sum of Selection for Hand	Number of Scoring 'Turn-Up' Cards	Weighted Average Increase in Score
18A	6, 6, 7, 7, 8, 8	6, 7, 7, 8 (12)	28	22	2.48
		6, 8 (0)		14	0.74
18B	6, 6, 7, 7, 8, 8	6, 7, 8, 8 (12)	29	22	2.30
		6, 7 (0)		18	1.00
Comment: The dealer should keep selection 18B because there is a better chance of getting a good score from the crib. If the (6, 7) are discarded there are six cards (four 5's and two 8's) amongst the 46 unknown cards with which they can form sequences whereas, if the (6, 8) are discarded by keeping selection 18A there are only two such cards (two 7's). With hands of this type there will be only a small difference in the weighted average increase in the score due to the 'Turn-Up' card. The non-dealer should keep selection 18A because, of the two possible selections which give the maximum score without the aid of the 'Turn-Up' card, it provides the best balking cards to the crib.					
19A	7, 7, 8, 8, 9, 9	7, 7, 8, 9 (12)	31	18	1.96
		8, 9 (0)		14	0.83
19B	7, 7, 8, 8, 9, 9	7, 8, 8, 9 (12)	32	14	1.78
		7, 9 (0)		10	0.57
Comment: The dealer should keep selection 19A as the discards have the better chance of scoring in the crib for similar reasons to those given in the comments for example 18. Likewise the non-dealer should keep selection 19B.					
20A	4, 4, 5, 6, 6, K	4, 4, 5, 6 (12)	19	42	3.39
		6, K (0)		12	0.52
20B	4, 4, 5, 6, 6, K	4, 5, 6, 6 (12)	21	34	3.22
		4, K (0)		12	0.52
Comment: Either player should keep selection 20A. There is little difference in the scoring qualities of the discards.					

Quiz on unusual hands

21. (5 + 6 + 7 + 7 + 8 + Q)	**24.** (2 + 2 + 3 + 3 + 4 + 4)
22. (A + A + 2 + 2 + 3 + 3)	**25.** (A + 2 + 3 + 3 + 4 + 7)
23. (A + A + 2 + 3 + 3 + 7)	**26.** (2 + 2 + 3 + 3 + 6 + 6)

Answers to quiz

It is unlikely that a player will receive these or similar hands, but would be lucky to do so. Low cards predominate in examples 22 to 26 and because no '10' cards are contained in any of them all sixteen are amongst the possible 'Turn-Up' cards. It follows that any combination of cards which add up to 5 will have a marked effect on the weighted average increase in the score, and the more of these combinations there are the greater this effect will be. When two or more selections have the same number of combinations which add up to 5 then, in order to choose the selection for which the 'Turn-Up' card will be most beneficial, it is necessary to find the one which, for the cards retained in the hand, has the greatest number of combinations which can form 15/2 with any of the possible 'Turn-Up' cards. In these unusual cases the 'Turn-Up' card need not be most beneficial to the selection of four cards with the lowest numerical sum.

Table 6.7

Unusual Hands

Effect of 'Turn-Up' card on score from cards retained and discarded

Example	Cards Received	Selection for Hand and Discards	Numerical Sum of Selection for Hand	Number of Scoring 'Turn-Up' Cards	Weighted Average Increase in Score
21A	5, 6, 7, 7, 8, Q	6, 7, 7, 8 (12)	28	23	2.87
		5, Q (2)		18	1.04
21B	5, 6, 7, 7, 8, Q	5, 6, 7, 7 (8)	25	46	3.78
		8, Q (0)		11	0.48

Comment: The dealer should keep selection 21A with a guaranteed score of 14 points from the hand and crib.
By choosing selection 21A the non-dealer scores a net 10 points (12 points from the hand minus 2 donated to the crib). However, there is a good chance that further points will be lost if one of the dealer's discards or the 'Turn-Up' card is a '10' card. On the other hand if selection 21B is chosen there is a guaranteed 8 points from the hand and good balking cards are put into the crib. Unless the position on the cribbage board dictates otherwise selection 21B is the better choice.

22A	A, A, 2, 2, 3, 3	A, A, 2, 3	(8)	7	34	3.09
		2, 3	(0)		26	1.26
22B	A, A, 2, 2, 3, 3	A, 2, 2, 3	(8)	8	38	3.96
		A, 3	(0)		6	0.30
22C	A, A, 2, 2, 3, 3	A, 2, 3, 3	(8)	9	42	3.61
		A, 2	(0)		6	0.30

Comment: The dealer should keep selection 22A because the (2 + 3) combination has a good chance of scoring in the crib.
For that reason, the non-dealer should not keep 22A and, of the other two choices, 22B rather than 22C should be chosen. With the former there are three ways in which the cards in the hand can be combined to add up to 5, whereas with the latter there are only two.

23A	A, A, 2, 3, 3, 7	A, A, 2, 3	(8)	7	35	3.26
		3, 7	(0)		13	0.57
23B	A, A, 2, 3, 3, 7	A, 2, 3, 3	(8)	9	42	3.74
		A, 7	(0)		9	0.52

Comment: Both players should keep 23B. Selections 23A and 23B both have two ways in which the cards retained can combine to add up to 5, but 23B has eight ways of forming 15/2 with the 'Turn-Up' cards. With 23A there are only five ways and so both players should choose 23B as there is little difference in the scoring potential of either set of discards.

For selection 23A the ways are:
(2 + 3) with the 'Turn-Up' a '10' card
(A + A + 3) with the 'Turn-Up' a '10' card
(A + 2 + 3) with the 'Turn-Up' a 9 (twice)
(A + A + 2 + 3) with the 'Turn-Up' an 8

For selection 23B the ways are:
(2 + 3) with the 'Turn-Up' a '10' card (twice)
(A + 2 + 3) with the 'Turn-Up' a 9 (twice)
(3 + 3) with the 'Turn-Up' a 9
(A + 3 + 3) with the 'Turn-Up' an 8
(2 + 3 + 3) with the 'Turn-Up' a 7
(A + 2 + 3 + 3) with the 'Turn-Up' a 6

24A	2, 2, 3, 3, 4, 4	2, 2, 3, 4	(8)	11	46	4.04
		3, 4	(0)		14	0.74
24B	2, 2, 3, 3, 4, 4	2, 3, 3, 4	(8)	12	46	4.22
		2, 4	(0)		10	0.48
24C	2, 2, 3, 3, 4, 4	2, 3, 4, 4	(8)	13	46	3.61
		2, 3	(0)		26	1.26

Comment: The dealer should keep selection 24C and discard the (2 + 3) combination and hope for a good score from the crib even though the hand retained only has one combination of cards adding up to 5, whereas with selections 24A and 24B the hands both have two. The reason is that three cards influence those added to the crib while only the 'Turn-Up' card can benefit the cards retained in hand. It is difficult for the non-dealer to choose between selections 24A and 24B. There is little difference in the number of ways of forming 15/2 with the 'Turn-Up' card (ten for selection 24A and eleven for 24B).
It is better for the non-dealer to keep selection 24B as there are only two 3's amongst the 46 'unknown' cards which can form a sequence with the (2, 4) discarded.

25A	A, 2, 3, 3, 4, 7	A, 2, 3, 3 (8)	9	42	3.87
		4, 7 (0)		10	0.57
25B	A, 2, 3, 3, 4, 7	2, 3, 3, 4 (8)	12	46	4.48
		A, 7 (0)		10	0.57

Comment: This is very similar to example 23 but is included in order to demonstrate the importance of the number of ways of forming 15/2 with the 'Turn-Up' card. The hands from selections 25A and 25B both have two combinations which add up to 5 and there is little difference in the quality of the cards discarded. Both players should keep selection 25B which has eleven ways of forming 15/2 with the possible 'Turn-Up' cards, whereas selection 25A has eight.

For selection 25A the ways are:
(2 + 3) with the 'Turn-Up' a '10' card (twice)
(3 + 3) with the 'Turn-Up' a 9
(A + 2 + 3) with the 'Turn-Up' a 9 (twice)
(A + 3 + 3) with the 'Turn-Up' an 8
(2 + 3 + 3) with the 'Turn-Up' a 7
(A + 2 + 3 + 3) with the 'Turn-Up' a 6

For selection 25B the ways are:
(2 + 3) with the 'Turn-Up' a '10' card (twice)
(3 + 3) with the 'Turn-Up' a 9
(2 + 4) with the 'Turn-Up' an 8
(3 + 4) with the 'Turn-Up' an 8 (twice)
(2 + 3 + 3) with the 'Turn-Up' a 7
(2 + 3 + 4) with the 'Turn-Up' a 6 (twice)
(3 + 3 + 4) with the 'Turn-Up' a 5
(2 + 3 + 3 + 4) with the 'Turn-Up' a 3

26A	2, 2, 3, 3, 6, 6	2, 2, 3, 3 (4)	10	44	6.26
		6, 6 (2)		8	0.61
26B	2, 2, 3, 3, 6, 6	3, 3, 6, 6 (8)	18	8	1.48
		2, 2 (2)		2	0.17

Comment: This example deserves special comment.

There is a difference of 4 points between the scores from the hands of selections 26A and 26B and, if the guidance already given is followed, selection 26B should be chosen by both the dealer and the non-dealer.

However, in this case it does not pay to do so. With selection 26A only 4 points are scored from the cards retained in hand but there is a weighted average increase in the score of 6.28, giving a potential total score of (4 + 6.26) = 10.26.

On the other hand with selection 26B, for which 8 points are scored from the cards retained in hand, the weighted average increase is only 1.48, so that the most likely potential score is (8 + 1.48) = 9.48. In this particular case it is better, *for both players,* to hold four cards which do not give the maximum score without the aid of the 'Turn-Up' card. It must be emphasised this is a single example out of more than 2,000,000 six-card combinations which are possible in six-card two-handed cribbage and the probability of getting this particular hand is very low.

MAXIMISING THE INCREASE IN THE SCORE FROM THE 'TURN-UP' CARD

Six cards received from the dealer

Summary of advice to DEALER

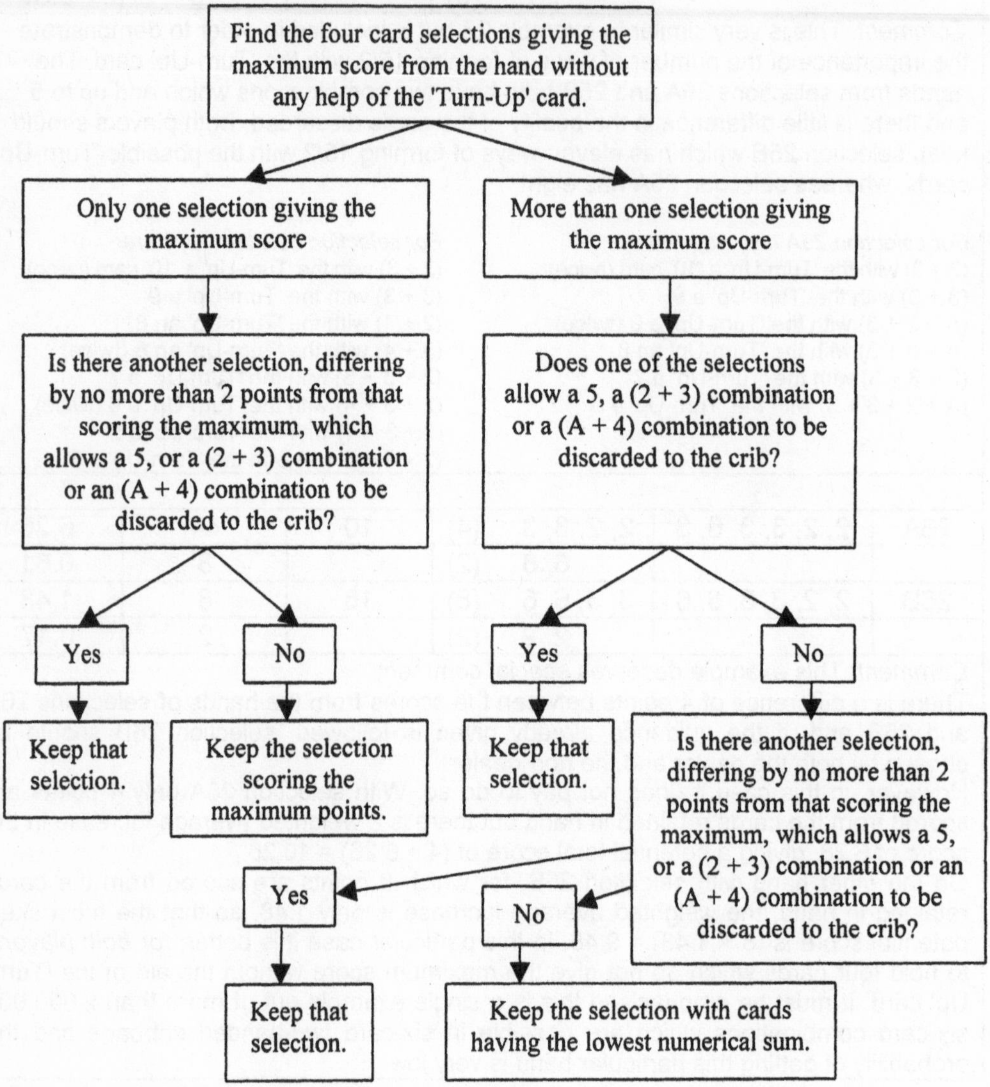
Find the four card selections giving the maximum score from the hand without any help of the 'Turn-Up' card.
Only one selection giving the maximum score
More than one selection giving the maximum score
Is there another selection, differing by no more than 2 points from that scoring the maximum, which allows a 5, or a (2 + 3) combination or an (A + 4) combination to be discarded to the crib?
Does one of the selections allow a 5, a (2 + 3) combination or a (A + 4) combination to be discarded to the crib?
Yes
No
Yes
No
Keep that selection.
Keep the selection scoring the maximum points.
Keep that selection.
Is there another selection, differing by no more than 2 points from that scoring the maximum, which allows a 5, or a (2 + 3) combination or an (A + 4) combination to be discarded to the crib?
Yes
No
Keep that selection.
Keep the selection with cards having the lowest numerical sum.

MAXIMISING THE INCREASE IN THE SCORE FROM THE 'TURN-UP' CARD

Six cards received from the dealer

Summary of advice to NON-DEALER

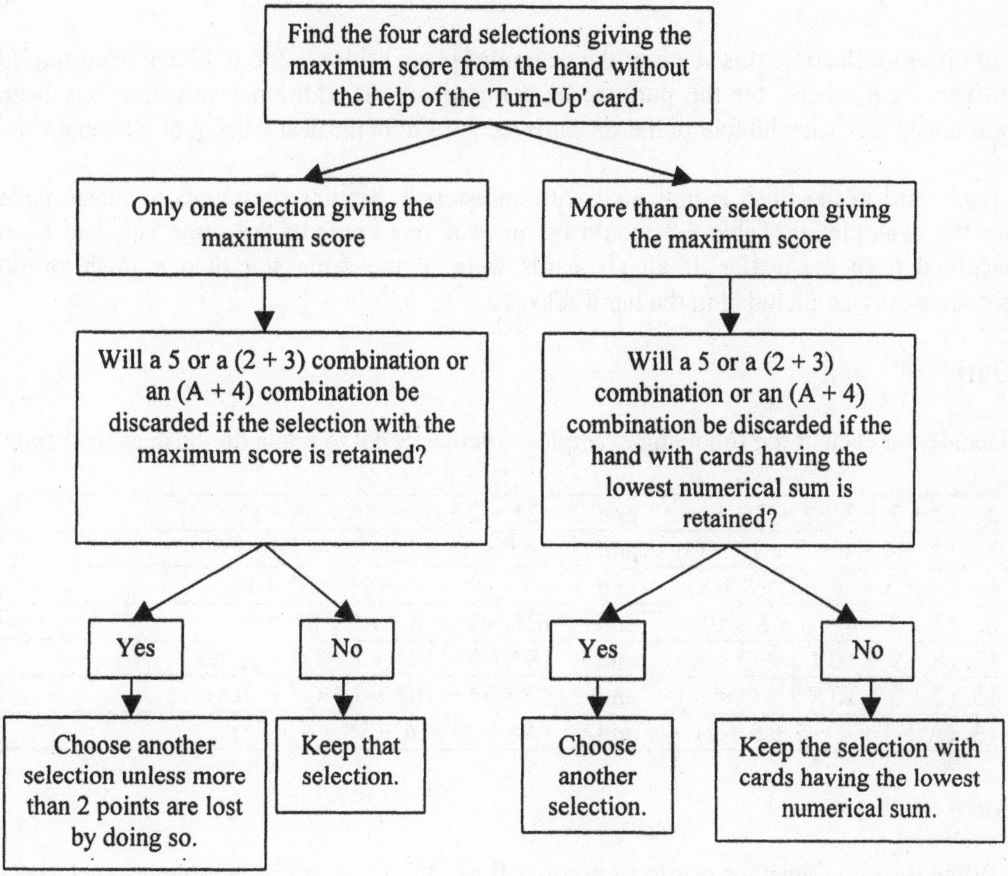
Find the four card selections giving the maximum score from the hand without the help of the 'Turn-Up' card.
Only one selection giving the maximum score
More than one selection giving the maximum score
Will a 5 or a (2 + 3) combination or an (A + 4) combination be discarded if the selection with the maximum score is retained?
Will a 5 or a (2 + 3) combination or an (A + 4) combination be discarded if the hand with cards having the lowest numerical sum is retained?
Yes
No
Yes
No
Choose another selection unless more than 2 points are lost by doing so.
Keep that selection.
Choose another selection.
Keep the selection with cards having the lowest numerical sum.

Scoring from flushes

When dealt four or more cards of the same suit a player has to decide whether it is beneficial to keep a flush as the hand. First check whether more points can be obtained in other ways.

In order to illustrate this some of the examples from Tables 6.2 to 6.7 have been reused in Table 6.8 where, for the purpose of comparison, an additional selection has been introduced for each with four of the six cards received from the dealer being of the same suit.

Each card in the flush is indicated with an asterisk. Similar comments to those made for the examples in Table 6.8 would be made if five cards of the same suit had been received from the dealer. If all six cards were of the same suit then a flush would automatically be included in the hand selected.

Quiz

Decide, for each of the following examples, whether or not to retain the flush as the hand.

2. (2 + 2 + 3 + 5 + 7 + 8)	and	(2* + 2 + 3* + 5* + 7* + 8)
3. (A + 4 + 6 + 7 + 10 + Q)	and	(A* + 4* + 6* + 7* + 10 + Q)
5. (A + 5 + 6 + 7 + 8 + 8)	and	(A + 5* + 6* + 7* + 8* + 8)
6. (2 + 3 + 6 + 6 + 8 + 9)	and	(2* + 3* + 6 + 6* + 8* + 9)
12. (8 + 9 + 10 + J + Q + K)	and	(8* + 9 + 10* + J + Q* + K*)
13. (2 + 3 + 10 + J + Q + K)	and	(2 + 3* + 10* + J + Q* + K*)
15. (A + 3 + 4 + 5 + 6 + 7)	and	(A* + 3* + 4 + 5* + 6 + 7*)

Answers to quiz

When deciding whether or not to retain a flush, the same advice applies as was given for the other examples. However, both players should exploit any additional ways of getting the maximum score from the hand and, if the dealer, from the crib as well. Because 4 points, and possibly 5, are scored from a flush it is not necessary to make comparison with any other selection which scores less than this.

Every card in a flush will be of different rank and, therefore, compared with any hand containing a pair of cards, there is a better chance of increasing the score by pairing the 'Turn-Up' card. If the cards in the flush are suitably spaced there is also a better chance of scoring from sequences.

Table 6.8					
Four of the cards received are of the same suit					
Effect of 'Turn-Up' card on score from cards retained and discarded					
Example	**Cards Received**	**Selection for Hand and Discards**	**Numerical Sum of Selection for Hand**	**Number of Scoring 'Turn-Up' Cards**	**Weighted Average Increase in Score**
2A	2, 2, 3, 5, 7, 8	2, 2, 5, 8 (6)	17	34	2.17
		3, 7 (0)		12	0.52
2C	2*, 2, 3*, 5*, 7*, 8	2*, 3*, 5*, 7* (6)	17	42	4.20
		2, 8 (0)		11	0.48
Comment: Both players should keep selection 2C. Because this selection contains both a 5 and a (2 + 3) combination, the weighted average increase in the score due to the 'Turn-Up' card should be much greater than with selection 2A .					
3A	A, 4, 6, 7, 10, Q	A, 4,10, Q (4)	25	24	2.26
		6, 7 (0)		22	1.30
3C	A*, 4*, 6*, 7*, 10, Q	A*, 4*, 6*, 7* (4)	18	46	3.50
		10, Q (0)		14	0.87
Comment: Both players should keep selection 3C. These cards have the lowest possible numerical sum and, therefore, the weighted average increase in the score due to the 'Turn-Up' card should be greater than that from any other selection. If it were not for the flush selection 3C would not be considered as it contains no other way of scoring points.					
5A	A, 5, 6, 7, 8, 8	6, 7, 8, 8 (12)	29	22	2.61
		A, 5 (0)		26	1.13
5C	A, 5*, 6*, 7*, 8*, 8	5*, 6*, 7*, 8* (10)	26	46	3.52
		A, 8 (0)		11	0.48
Comment: The dealer should not keep the flush but should choose selection 5A which scores the maximum without the aid of the 'Turn-Up' card and also enables a 5 to be discarded to the crib. The non-dealer should keep selection 5C which only scores 2 points less than the maximum and also avoids having to discard a 5 to the crib. Moreover, because selection 5C has a lower numerical sum than selection 5A, there is a better chance of scoring via the 'Turn-Up' card.					

6A	2, 3, 6, 6, 8, 9	6, 6, 8, 9 (6)	29	23	2.39
		2, 3 (0)		30	1.48
6B	2, 3, 6, 6, 8, 9	2, 3, 6, 6 (4)	17	39	3.09
		8, 9 (0)		16	1.04
6C	2*, 3*, 6, 6*, 8*, 9	2*, 3* , 6*, 8* (4)	19	46	3.54
		6, 9 (2)		5	0.43

Comment: It is difficult for the dealer to choose between selections 6A and 6C both of which guarantee 6 points. The former allows a (2 + 3) combination to be discarded whilst the latter has the lower numerical sum and also has four different cards as the hand. Selection 6C should be chosen as it has the better chance of scoring both via the 'Turn-Up' card and by pegging.
Only 2 points (net) are scored if the non-dealer keeps the flush. Selection 6B should be chosen for the reasons given in Table 6.2.

12A	8, 9, 10, J, Q, K	8, 9, 10, J (4)	37	27	2.41
		Q, K (0)		13	0.80
12C	8*, 9, 10*, J, Q*, K*	8*, 10*, Q*, K* (4)	38	26	1.87
		9, J (0)		17	0.80

Comment: Both players should choose selection 12A for which there are more possible 'Turn-Up' cards able to form sequences with the cards retained in the hand (19 cards in the case of selection 12A but only 6 with selection 12C). The discards from these selections are of similar quality.

13A	2, 3, 10, J, Q, K	2, 3, 10, J (4)	25	34	2.89
		Q, K (0)		13	0.80
13C	2, 3, 10, J, Q, K	10, J, Q, K (4)	40	20	2.35
		2, 3 (0)		26	1.30
13D	2, 3*, 10*, J, Q*, K*	3*, 10*, Q*, K* (4)	33	22	1.89
		2, J (0)		13	0.57

Comment: The dealer should reject the flush and choose selection 13C for the reasons given in Table 6.4.
The non-dealer should also reject the flush but should choose selection 13A for the reasons given in Table 6.4.

15A	A, 3, 4, 5, 6, 7	3, 4, 5, 6 (6)	18	46	3.85
		A, 7 (0)		10	0.57
15C	A*, 3*, 4, 5*, 6, 7*	A*, 3*, 5*, 7* (6)	16	46	3.37
		4, 6 (0)		13	0.76

Comment: Both players should choose selection 15A and hope for an 8-point increase in the score due to the 'Turn-Up' card being either a 3, 4, 5 or 6, knowing that there are twelve such cards amongst the 46 'unknown' cards. 5 additional points are the maximum that can be scored via the 'Turn-Up' card if selection 15C is chosen.

Increasing the score from the crib

Whereas it is theoretically possible to calculate the probabilities of scoring combinations between any four of the cards received at each deal and the 'Turn-Up' card, and by using the procedure outlined above to aim for the maximum number of points from the cards retained in hand, a similar approach cannot be used for scoring combinations between the cards in the crib. The dealer will try to discard with the aim of getting the maximum score from the crib, but the non-dealer will try to balk the crib.

The players' actions are independent of each other and it would be pointless to try to use a mathematical approach for assessing any increase due to the interaction of the discards. However, there are a number of guide-lines, which can be used by both players when selecting the cards to give to the crib. While most of these have already been discussed, a somewhat more quantitative approach is given here.

There are four cards of each rank in a pack of cards and, because of this, there is a 1-in-13 chance that a card of a specified rank will be discarded *randomly* to the crib. If the players *select* the discards then the chance that a card of a specified rank will be discarded will be either greater or smaller than that.

Except in the final stages of a game, experience has shown that, in order to score the maximum number of points from the cards received at each deal, the overriding consideration, when selecting the discards, was to obtain the greatest score from the cards retained in hand. Although the non-dealer should always try to avoid putting cards into the crib which might become part of scoring combinations, a balance should be struck between what are certain or likely points gained from the hand versus possible points lost in the crib. Similarly the dealer should put only potentially good cards into the crib when they do not unduly jeopardise the certain and potential score from the cards in hand.

By making an analysis of which cards were discarded from a very large number of games it has been possible to arrange the cards in order of the frequency with which they were chosen as discards. The results from the last deals from each game have been excluded from the analysis because, as explained earlier, different discarding criteria tend to apply in the final stages of a game. Discarding is a subjective process and, over a large number of deals, no two players will discard in exactly the same way. Therefore no set of frequencies relating to the discards from groups of cards should ever be taken as an absolute guide.

However, using the results from such an analysis helps the dealer to maximise, and the non-dealer to minimise, the score from the crib. The results of the analysis, expressed as percentage frequencies of cards being discarded to the crib, are shown in Table 6.9. Because of the inherent inaccuracies, and also for the sake of simplicity, the percentages have been rounded off to whole numbers. For easy comparison of the discards from the dealer and the non-dealer, the frequencies have been arranged in decreasing order of their occurrence.

Table 6.9

Frequencies of Cards being Discarded to the Crib

% frequency	13	12	9	9	9	8	7	7	6	5	5	5	4
Dealer	Q	K	2	A	8	9	10	3	7	J	4	5	6
% frequency	14	12	11	11	9	8	7	7	6	6	5	4	0
Non-dealer	K	Q	2	A	10	3	J	9	8	6	5	7	5

Table 6.9 does *not* give any direct information relating to the frequency of either player choosing to discard certain pairs of cards, such as (2 + 3) and (A + 4), which are likely to become involved in scoring combinations, but some helpful information can be deduced. For obvious reasons the *non-dealer* should avoid discarding such combinations, but the results show that, although desirable, the *dealer* is only able to use them on infrequent occasions. Thus, at the very best, there is only a 7% frequency for a (2 + 3) combination, and a 5% frequency for a (A + 4) combination being discarded by the dealer.

Such frequencies are low because it is generally best to adopt a cautious approach and to keep those cards in hand which are most likely to score the most and, in the long run, these tactics will usually be beneficial. If a gambling approach is adopted throughout the whole game the frequencies that such pairs will be discarded by the dealer increases. When choosing discards each player should try to gauge the tactics used by the other.

A number of points arise from the frequencies shown in Table 6.9:

1. There is little difference between the most probable discards from the *dealer* and the *non-dealer*, both players favouring either a King or a Queen.

2. The need to keep scoring combinations in hand often forces *both players* to discard Kings and Queens. The *dealer* can sometimes use this to his advantage. For example, if the cards received by the *dealer* are 2, 3, 4, 7, 10, Q, he should discard (7 + Q) rather than (7 + 10) knowing that the *non-dealer* is more likely to discard a Q than a 10.

3. The *non-dealer* should *never* discard a 5 and should avoid (2 + 3) and (A + 4) combinations.

4. There is about a 40% chance that the *non-dealer* will discard a '10' card. The *dealer* should, therefore, discard a 5 or (2 + 3) or (A + 4) whenever possible. The opportunity to discard a 5 is infrequent because, even if there is one amongst the cards dealt, it is generally better to keep it in the hand in order to score the maximum number of guaranteed points. Knowing this, the *non-dealer* can feel fairly safe when discarding one '10' card, but it is wise to try to avoid discarding two, especially if they are of adjacent rank, or are separated by one rank, because of the danger of forming sequences with the dealer's discards.

5. Although the differences in the frequencies are small the *non-dealer* is less likely than the *dealer* to discard 7's, 8's and 9's to the crib and it is very unlikely that the non-dealer will put two of them into the crib. The *dealer* should bear this in mind and if he chooses such cards as discards he should be aware that there is likely to be more chance of their combining with the 'Turn-Up' card than with the discards from the *non-dealer.*

6. Because other cards are more likely to help with the score in the hand, there is a greater than random frequency of both Aces and 2's being discarded by *both players.* The results in Table 9 have been obtained from the majority of hands in each game where points are required from every aspect, the pegging, the hand and the crib. If pegging becomes the most important aspect, as often happens in the later stages of a game, Aces and 2's are much less likely to be discarded by either player. For example, if the *non-dealer* is seen to need a large score by pegging in order to have a chance of winning the game, the *dealer* will expect his opponent to have kept low cards in hand and, therefore, should not expect low cards from the *non-dealer* to be of any help to the score from the crib.

Chapter 7

FIVE-CARD CRIBBAGE

This is the original game and, although the six-card game is now more popular, the five-card game still has its adherents and many people play both forms. More skill is required in order to play the original game well because, with only five cards received at each deal, it is more difficult to choose those which have the greatest scoring potential. The main differences between the two games are as follows:

1. Instead of 121 points for six-card cribbage only 61 points are required to complete a game which, if a traditional cribbage board is used, is once round the board and into the game hole.

2. After the cards have been cut to decide which player should be the first to deal, the loser of the cut should peg three points, sometimes called *three for last.* These points, which are only scored once, compensate for the fact that the odds of winning are slightly in favour of the player dealing first.

3. Five cards are dealt to each player and both discard two to the crib. The players' hands therefore only contain three cards but, as in the six-card game, the crib contains four.

4. The play of the cards is the same as in the six-card game, but once the first 'Go' or '31' has been reached no further cards are played.

5. The scoring of the hands and crib follow the same rules as for the six-card game but because only three cards instead of four are held in each hand the average scores are lower. On the other hand the average score from the crib should be the same.

6. The rules for flushes are the same for both games.

7. A 'lurch' or double game can be claimed if a player wins before his opponent has scored 31 points.

Strategy and tactics in the five-card game

Most of the discussion given for the six-card game also applies here but, because of the low scoring nature of the five-card game, every extra single point gained during play can be of great importance. The approximate number of points, averaged and rounded off to whole numbers, which are likely to be scored from each deal is as follows:

	Dealer	Non-Dealer
From the play	2	2
From the hand	4	4
From the crib	5	0
Total	**11**	**6**

On the basis of these figures seven deals should be required to complete a game. After the cards have been dealt, played and scored six times, the winner of the cut would have scored (3 x 11) + (3 x 6) = 51 points, and would require 61 – 51 = 10 points to win.

On the other hand the loser of the cut would have 3 + (3 x 11) + (3 x 6) = 54 points and would require 7 to win. This is one more than should, on average, be gained by the non-dealer from the cards received at the seventh deal. The non-dealer should therefore do everything possible to gain extra points from the previous deals and the dealer should try to prevent this happening.

The crib provides a greater proportion of the total points available in the five-card than in the six-card game. Therefore, relatively speaking, the crib is more valuable than the hand. Whenever possible the non-dealer should always discard to try to balk the crib even if, at times, by doing so there is a reduction in the chance of the cards retained in his hand combining with the 'Turn-Up' card.

It is even wiser than in the six-card game for the non-dealer to keep cards in hand which offer the best chance of scoring by pegging as the cards are played. Similarly, irrespective of which are retained, the cards should be played with even greater care so that the chance of the opponent scoring is reduced to a minimum. Once the first 'Go' has been reached no further cards can be played and it is probable that not all of the three cards from the hand will be played. Each player should therefore be careful in choosing which cards it is most advantageous *not* to play as well as choosing those that should be played.

Flushes are more important and are kept more frequently than in the six-card game. There is a greater probability that three out of five rather than four out of six cards dealt will be of the same suit. Moreover it is more likely that a player will choose to keep a flush because, in a low scoring game, a score of 3 for a flush, or 4 if the 'Turn-Up' card is of that suit, is of greater significance than in the six-card game. For a flush to be counted in the crib the same rule applies as in the six-card game, i.e., all four cards and the 'Turn-Up' card must be of the same suit.

Increase in the score from the hand due to the 'Turn-Up' card

When discarding to the crib and trying for the maximum help from the 'Turn-Up' card to the score in hand the five-card game, as opposed to the six-card game, features two main differences which both players should consider very carefully. Firstly, on the basis of average scores, more points are available from the crib than from the hands and, secondly, only three cards are kept in the hand. Because of the latter a hand cannot contain both a pair and a sequence and a double sequence can only be formed with the help of the 'Turn-Up' card. The effect of the 'Turn-Up' card is, in many ways, more important than in the six-card game and the ability to judge the best cards to retain is critical to a player's success.

In the six-card game it has been shown that, with very few exceptions, it is best to keep the four cards in hand which have the maximum score and, if there is a choice in the ways of doing this, to select from the six received from the dealer the four which have the lowest numerical sum. By doing this the effect of the 'Turn-Up' card will be most beneficial because, with a hand of four cards, the selection chosen will, generally, have more ways in which the cards can combine with the 'Turn-Up' card to score 15/2 and to form sequences.

This is not true in the five-card game where only three cards are retained as the hand. If there is more than one selection which will give the maximum score without the help of the 'Turn-Up' card, it is not necessarily best to keep that with the lowest numerical sum, although this will sometimes be the case. In addition, compared with the six-card game, more care is required of both players when discarding to the crib because, relative to the hand, it has greater scoring potential. Furthermore, with only one count to 'Go', the method of discarding may be influenced by the fact that some of the cards from the hand may not be played during the pegging stage. Because of these reasons the five-card game requires greater skill and is the more challenging game even though it is less frequently played.

The procedures below are suggested as guidance for finding that selection for which the 'Turn-Up' card is likely to be most beneficial to the hand and, if dealer, to the crib as well. Because of the extra constraints imposed on the non-dealer separate guidance is given for the two players. It is fairly common for no score to be possible from any selection of three cards from the five received; examples are therefore included for those hands which score without the help of the 'Turn-Up' card and for those that do not. When no score is possible it is more important that both players should remember that, whereas the score from the cards retained in hand can be increased only by the 'Turn-Up' card, those discarded will combine with the opponent's discards. The players should choose their selections accordingly. This often means that the dealer does not keep the selection which offers the best chance of scoring from the hand and concentrates on the potential score from the crib.

In the section below, following each part of the advice on discarding, there are Tables of illustrative examples. Only those selections needed to illustrate the advice regarding the effect of the 'Turn-Up' card are given in the Tables 7.1 to 7.11.

For all of the examples used in those Tables it has been assumed that it is not possible to retain a flush as the hand. The extra considerations that are necessary when the retention of a flush as the hand is a possibility are illustrated and discussed in Table 7.12.

Selection Procedure

Deals for which only one selection gives the maximum score for the hand

Advice to the dealer

Keep the selection which scores the maximum number of points without the aid of the 'Turn-Up' card unless there is another selection, with a score differing by not more than 2 points from the maximum and which gives a much better chance of a high score from the crib.

Advice to the non-dealer

Keep the selection which scores the maximum number of points without the aid of the 'Turn-Up' card, those points being the points from the hand minus any which have been donated to the crib, unless, by doing so, it is necessary to discard either a 5 or a (2 + 3) or an (A + 4) combination and the score from the selection retained is 3 or less. If so choose another selection. Keep the selection with the maximum score if it is more than 3 points greater than from any other and, if necessary, discard a 5 or (2 +3) or (A +4) combination as it unlikely than any extra score from the crib will be as great as that lost by not keeping the selection with the maximum score.

Quiz

Assume, for each of the following examples, that the same set of cards was received by (a) the dealer and (b) the non-dealer. Which cards should be retained in hand?

The answers to the quiz are given in the authors' comments in Table 7.1

1. (A + 4 + 5 + 8 + 9)	**4.** (2 + 3 + 8 + 9 + 10)
2. (2 + 5 + 10 + J + Q)	**5.** (2 + 3 + 5 + 10 + K)
3. (3 + 5 + 7 + 7 + 8)	

Answers to quiz

Table 7.1					
Only one selection giving the maximum score					
Effect of 'Turn-Up' card on score from cards retained and discarded					
Example	**Cards Received**	**Selection for Hand and Discards**	**Numerical Sum of Selection for Hand**	**Number of Scoring 'Turn-Up' Cards**	**Weighted Average Increase in Score**
1A	A, 4, 5, 8, 9	A, 5, 9 (2)	15	29	1.62
		4, 8 (0)		14	0.60
1B	A, 4, 5, 8, 9	5, 8, 9 (0)	22	40	2.21
		A, 4 (0)		22	0.94
1C	A, 4, 5, 8, 9	A, 8, 9 (0)	18	24	1.53
		4, 5 (0)		30	1.62
Comment: The dealer should keep either 1B or 1C, even though they score 2 points less than 1A, and discard the (A + 4) or (4 + 5) in the hope that the 'Turn-Up' card and/or one of the opponent's discards will be a '10' card. On balance it is better to keep 1B because any 'Turn-Up' card other than a 3 or a 4 will increase the score in hand by at least 2 points. The non-dealer should keep selection 1A which gives the maximum guaranteed score and avoids having to discard either a 5 or an (A + 4) combination.					
2A	2, 5, 10 J, Q	5, 10, J (4)	25	20	1.64
		2, Q (0)		13	0.55
2B	2, 5, 10, J, Q	10, J, Q (3)	30	20	1.51
		2, 5 (0)		23	0.98
Comment: The dealer should keep selection 2B, with one less point than the maximum, and discard the 5 in the hope of obtaining a good score from the crib. The non-dealer should keep selection 2A, which has the maximum score and allows the best balking cards to be given to the crib.					
3A	3, 5, 7, 7, 8	7, 7, 8 (6)	22	17	1.83
		3, 5 (0)		28	1.28
3B	3, 5, 7,7, 8	5, 7, 8 (2)	20	39	2.13
		3, 7 (0)		11	0.47
Comment: The dealer should keep selection 3A which gives the maximum score without the help of the 'Turn-Up' card and allows a 5 to be discarded to the crib. The non-dealer should keep 3A even though a 5 has to be discarded. It is unlikely that any extra score from the dealer's crib will outweigh the 4 points lost if 3B were chosen.					

4A	2, 3, 8, 9, 10	8, 9, 10 (3)	27	25	1.64
		2, 3 (0)		29	1.40
4B	2, 3, 8, 9, 10	2, 3, 10 (2)	15	33	1.96
		8, 9 (0)		17	1.04
Comment: The dealer should keep selection 4A, which scores the maximum, and discard the (2 + 3) combination to the crib. The non-dealer should keep selection 4B even though, relative to 4A, one point is lost by not discarding the (2 + 3) combination.					
5A	2, 3, 5, 10, K	5, 10, K (4)	25	17	1.23
		2, 3 (0)		28	1.36
5B	2, 3, 5, 10, K	2, 3, 5 (0)	10	39	2.64
		10, K (0)		9	0.51
5C	2, 3, 5, 10, K	2, 3, 10 (2)	15	31	1.87
		5, K (2)		17	0.98
Comment: Selections 5A and 5C both guarantee 4 points, the former scoring only from the hand and the latter scoring 2 from the hand and 2 from the crib. The dealer should choose selection 5C because the cards retained have the better chance of combining with the 'Turn-Up' card. In addition (5 + K) are the best discards because, of the '10' cards, a King is the most likely to be discarded by the non-dealer. The non-dealer should keep selection 5A even though, by doing so, a (2 + 3) combination must be discarded. It would be unlikely for the dealer to gain as many points from the crib as the 4 lost if either selection 5B or 5C were chosen.					

DEALS FOR WHICH TWO OR MORE SELECTIONS GIVE THE MAXIMUM SCORE FOR THE HAND

In the six-card game, when there is more than one selection giving the maximum score, choosing the one with the cards which have the lowest numerical sum is the recommended strategy. This is not necessarily best in the five-card game. Increasing the size of the hand from three to four cards simplifies the selection of the hand which is most likely to give the maximum score and it therefore follows that the five-card game is more difficult to play well.

The following procedure is recommended as a help when choosing which three cards to retain and which two to discard. It is based on the different ways in which the cards can combine with the 'Turn-Up' card and with the other discards.

The examples in the Tables illustrate the selection procedure and, following each example, there are comments which relate to the actions that should be taken by both players for optimum strategy.

(a) One of the selections scoring the maximum contains a 5, the other not

Advice to the dealer: *Discard the 5 unless it is possible to discard either a (2 + 3) or an (A + 4) combination whilst maintaining the maximum score; if so, discard the combination.*

Advice to the non-dealer: *Keep the selection with the 5 but do not discard a (2 + 3) or an (A + 4). If necessary keep both the 5 and the combination even if points are lost in so doing.*

Quiz

Assume, for each of the following examples, that the same set of cards was received by (a) the dealer and (b) the non-dealer. Which cards should be retained in hand? The answers to the quiz are given in the authors' comments in Table 7.2.

6. (A + 2 + 4 + 5 + 9)	**7.** (A + 3 + 5 + 7 + 8)

Answers to quiz

Table 7.2

Deals for which more than one selection gives the maximum score

(a) (i) It is possible to discard a 5

Example	Cards Received	Selection for Hand and Discards	Numerical Sum of Selection for Hand	Number of Scoring 'Turn-Up' Cards	Weighted Average Increase in Score
6A	A, 2, 4, 5, 9	A, 5, 9 (2)	15	29	1.62
		2, 4 (0)		13	0.64
6B	A, 2, 4, 5, 9	2, 4, 9 (2)	15	17	1.19
		A, 5 (0)		25	1.06
6C	A, 2, 4, 5, 9	A, 4, 5 (0)	10	36	2.68
		2, 9 (0)		13	0.55
Comment: The dealer should keep selection 6B and discard the 5 to the crib and hope that at least one '10' card will be amongst the 'Turn-Up' card and the opponent's discards. The non-dealer should keep 6A and hold for the maximum points without discarding a 5. In the final stages of a game, if points from pegging are likely to be decisive, either player should consider whether to sacrifice 2 points from the hand and to choose selection 6C.					
7A	A, 3, 5, 7, 8	A, 7, 8 (2)	16	17	1.45
		3, 5 (0)		29	1.32
7B	A, 3, 5, 7, 8	3, 5, 7 (2)	15	36	2.09
		A, 8 (0)		13	0.55
Comment: The dealer should choose selection 7A and discard the 5 to the crib. The non-dealer should choose selection 7B and retain the 5 in hand.					

Quiz

Assume, for each of the following examples, that the same set of cards was received by (a) the dealer and (b) the non-dealer. Which cards should be retained in hand?

The answers to the quiz are given in the authors' comments in Table 7.3.

8. (A + 4 + 5 + 8 + 10)	**9.** (2 + 3 + 5 + 9 + 10)

Answers to quiz

Table 7.3					
Deals for which more than one selection gives the maximum score					
(a) (ii) It is possible to discard either a 5 or a (2 + 3) or an (A + 4) combination					
Example	Cards Received	Selection for Hand and Discards	Numerical Sum of Selection for Hand	Number of Scoring 'Turn-Up' Cards	Weighted Average Increase in Score
8A	A, 4, 5, 8, 10	5, 8, 10 (2)	23	33	1.74
		A, 4 (0)		21	0.89
8B	A, 4, 5, 8, 10	A, 4, 10 (2)	15	21	1.40
		5, 8 (0)		29	1.23
8C	A, 4, 5, 8, 10	A, 4, 5 (0)	10	36	2.64
		8, 10 (0)		17	0.81
Comment: The dealer should keep selection 8A and discard the (A + 4) combination. The non-dealer should keep selection 8C and put the best balking cards into the dealer's crib although 2 points are lost in doing so. There is a good chance that the points lost will be recovered via the 'Turn-Up' card.					
9A	2, 3, 5, 9, 10	5, 9, 10 (2)	24	33	2.00
		2, 3 (0)		29	1.40
9B	2, 3, 5, 9, 10	2, 3, 10 (2)	15	32	1.91
		5, 9 (0)		29	1.23
9C	2, 3, 5, 9, 10	2, 3, 5 (0)	10	40	2.72
		9, 10 (0)		21	1.06
Comment: The dealer should keep selection 9A and discard the (2 + 3) combination. The non-dealer should keep selection 9C and put the best balking cards into the dealer's crib although 2 points are lost by so doing. There is a good chance that the points lost will be recovered via the 'Turn-Up' card.					

(b) One of the selections scoring the maximum contains either a pair of cards of the same rank or a (7 + 8) or a (6 + 9) combination

Advice to the dealer: *If the fifth card, with the help of the 'Turn-Up' card, can join with the combination to form a sequence, discard the pair; if the fifth card cannot form part of sequence, discard the combination.*

Advice to the non-dealer: *Keep the combination and one card from the pair.*

Quiz

Assume, for each of the following examples, that the same set of cards was received by (a) the dealer and (b) the non-dealer. Which cards should be retained in hand?

The answers to the quiz are given in the authors' comments in Table 7.4.

10. (4 + 4 + 6 + 8 + 9)	**12.** (4 + 4 + 6 + 9 + K)
11. (2 + 2 + 7 + 8 + K)	

Answers to quiz

Table 7.4

Deals for which more than one selection gives the maximum score

(b) One of the selections scoring the maximum contains either a pair of cards of the same rank or a (7 + 8) or a (6 +9) combination

Example	Cards Received	Selection for Hand and Discards		Numerical Sum of Selection for Hand	Number of Scoring 'Turn-Up' Cards	Weighted Average Increase in Score
10A	4, 4, 6, 8, 9	6, 8, 9	(2)	23	21	1.57
		4, 4	(2)		6	0.34
10B	4, 4, 6, 8, 9	4, 4, 8	(2)	16	13	0.98
		6, 9	(2)		6	0.51
10C	4, 4, 6, 8, 9	4, 6, 9	(2)	19	16	1.19
		4, 8	(0)		13	0.55

Comment: The dealer should keep selection 10A, but if, in the final stages of a game it is thought that the score from the crib will not be recorded, the dealer should keep selection 10C as it offers a better chance of scoring by pegging.
The non-dealer should keep selection 10C at any stage in the game.

11A	2, 2, 7, 8, K	7, 8, K (2)	25	21	1.32
		2,2 (2)		2	0.17
11B	2, 2, 7, 8, K	2, 2, K (2)	14	17	0.98
		7, 8 (2)		14	1.02
11C	2, 2, 7, 8, K	2, 7, 8 (2)	17	20	1.45
		2, K (0)		13	0.55
Comment: The dealer should keep selection 11B as the fifth card cannot, with the help of the 'Turn-Up' card, form part of a sequence with the (7 + 8) combination. In the final stages of the game the dealer should consider choosing selection 11C as it offers slightly more chance of scoring by pegging. The non-dealer should choose selection 11C at any stage of the game.					
12A	4, 4, 6, 9, K	6, 9, K (2)	25	13	0.81
		4, 4 (2)		6	0.34
12B	4, 4, 6, 9, K	4, 4, K (2)	18	17	0.98
		6, 9 (2)		6	0.51
12C	4, 4, 6, 9, K	4, 6, 9 (2)	19	16	1.19
		4, K (0)		13	0.55
Comment: The dealer should keep selection 12B as the fifth card cannot, with the help of the 'Turn-Up' card, form part of a sequence with a card from the (6 + 9) combination. In the final stages, if the score from the crib is unlikely to be recorded, the dealer should choose selection 12C. The non-dealer should choose selection 12C.					

(c) The cards received contain two sequences, each of three cards

Advice to the dealer: *Retain the sequence having the greatest chance of forming* 15/2 *and another sequence with the 'Turn-Up' card unless, by not keeping the maximum score from the hand, it is possible to discard with a good chance of recovering more points from the crib than have been lost from the hand.*

Advice to the non-dealer: *Retain the sequence having the greatest chance of forming* 15/2 *and another sequence with the 'Turn-Up' card.*

Quiz

Assume, for each of the following examples, that the same set of cards was received by (a) the dealer and (b) the non-dealer. Which cards should be retained in hand?

The answers to the quiz are given in the authors' comments in Table 7.5.

13. (6 + 7 + 8 + 9 + Q)	**14.** (A + 2 + 3 + 4 + 10)

Table 7.5

Deals for which more than one selection gives the maximum score

(c) The cards received contain two sequences, each of three cards

Example	Cards Received	Selection for Hand and Discards	Numerical Sum of Selection for Hand	Number of Scoring 'Turn-Up' Cards	Weighted Average Increase in Score
13A	6, 7, 8, 9, Q	6, 7, 8 (5)	21	24	1.83
		9, Q (0)		13	0.55
13B	6, 7, 8, 9, Q	7, 8, 9 (5)	24	16	1.49
		6, Q (0)		13	0.55

Comment: Both players should keep selection 13A which, ignoring the crib, can form 15/2 in combination with the 'Turn-Up' card in five ways. There are only three ways with 13B. The weighted average increase in the score will be greater with 13A.

For selection 13A the ways are:
6 with the 'Turn-Up' a 9
7 with the 'Turn-Up' an 8
8 with the 'Turn-Up' a 7
(6 + 7) with the 'Turn-Up' a 2
(6 + 8) with the 'Turn-Up' an A.

For selection 13B the ways are:
7 with the 'Turn-Up' an 8
8 with the 'Turn-Up' a 7
9 with the 'Turn-Up' a 6

Example	Cards Received	Selection for Hand and Discards	Numerical Sum of Selection for Hand	Number of Scoring 'Turn-Up' Cards	Weighted Average Increase in Score
14A	A, 2, 3, 4, 10	A, 2, 3 (3)	6	31	1.83
		4, 10 (0)		13	0.55
14B	A, 2, 3, 4, 10	2, 3, 4 (3)	9	43	2.26
		A, 10 (0)		13	0.55
14C	A, 2, 3, 4, 10	2, 3, 10 (2)	15	31	1.83
		A, 4 (0)		21	0.89
14D	A, 2, 3, 4, 10	A, 4, 10 (2)	15	25	1.44
		2, 3 (0)		27	1.28

Comment: For most deals in a game the dealer should choose either 14C or 14D. On balance it is better to choose 14D and to discard the (2 + 3) combination because it is more likely to score 15/2 and sequences in the crib. In the final stages of a game, if it is thought that the score from the crib will not be recorded, it is better to choose either selection 14A or 14B, both of which are good pegging hands.
The non-dealer should choose 14B which scores the maximum, provides good balking cards to the crib and gives more ways of forming 15/2 with the 'Turn-Up' card than 14A.

For selection 14A the ways are:
(2 + 3) with the 'Turn-Up' a '10' card
(A + 2 + 3) with the 'Turn-Up' a 9

For selection 14B the ways are:
(2 + 3) with the 'Turn-Up' a '10' card
(2 + 4) with the 'Turn-Up' a 9
(3 + 4) with the 'Turn-Up' an 8
(2 + 3 + 4) with the 'Turn-Up' a 6

(d) Two pairs are present but no sequences are possible with the 'Turn-Up' card

Advice to the dealer: *Keep the pair and the single card which offers the most ways of forming 15/2 with the 'Turn-Up' card and discard the other pair. If both selections give the same result, then choose that which combines with the most 'Turn-Up' cards to give a score. This will be the selection in which the three cards in hand have the lowest numerical sum.*

Advice to the non-dealer: *Keep one pair and one card from the other pair and, of the two selections, choose the one with most ways of forming 15/2 with the 'Turn-Up' card. If both have the same number of ways, choose that with the better chance of scoring by pegging.*

Quiz

Assume, for each of the following examples, that the same set of cards was received by (a) the dealer and (b) the non-dealer. Which cards should be retained in hand? The answers to the quiz are given in the authors' comments in Table 7.6.

15. (6 + 10 + 10 + K + K)	**17.** (A + A + 4 + 4 + 8)
16. (3 + 3 + 7 + 7 + 10)	

Answers to quiz

Table 7.6

Deals for which more than one selection gives the maximum score

(d) Two pairs present — No sequences possible

Example	Cards Received	Selection for Hand and Discards	Numerical Sum of Selection for Hand	Number of Scoring 'Turn-Up' Cards	Weighted Average Increase in Score
15A	6, 10, 10, K, K	6, 10, 10 (2)	26	13	0.81
		K, K (2)		6	0.51
15B	6, 10, 10, K, K	6, K, K (2)	26	13	0.81
		10, 10 (2)		6	0.51
15C	6, 10, 10, K, K	10, K, K (2)	30	8	0.77
		6, 10 (0)		13	0.55
15D	6, 10, 10, K, K	10, 10, K (2)	30	8	0.77
		6, K (0)		13	0.55

Comment: The dealer should choose selection 15A and discard the pair of kings. Given the choice the non-dealer will normally discard a K rather than a 10 as the former has less chance of forming a sequence in the crib.
Selections 15C and 15D both have three ways of forming 15/2 with the 'Turn-Up' card. There is little to choose between them and the non-dealer can choose either.

16A	3, 3, 7, 7, 10	3, 3, 10 (2)	16	17	0.98
		7, 7 (2)		10	0.68
16B	3, 3, 7, 7, 10	7, 7, 10 (2)	24	17	0.98
		3, 3 (2)		6	0.34
16C	3, 3, 7, 7, 10	3, 3, 7 (2)	13	20	1.11
		7, 10 (0)		13	0.55
16D	3, 3, 7, 7, 10	3, 7, 7 (2)	17	16	1.11
		3, 10 (0)		13	0.55

Comment: The dealer should keep selection 16A as the hand which has four ways of forming 15/2 with the 'Turn-Up' card, whereas selection 16B only has three ways. However, if in the final stages of the game the only hope of winning is by pegging as the cards are played, neither of these selections should be chosen.
It is better not to choose any of the selections shown but to keep (3 + 7 + 10) which, although having a zero count, should have a better chance of pairing the non-dealer's lead.

For selection 16A the ways are:
(3 + 3) with the 'Turn-Up' a 9,
10 with the 'Turn-Up' a 5 ,
(3 + 10) with the 'Turn-Up' a 2 (twice)

For selection 16B the ways are:
7 with the 'Turn-Up' an 8 (twice)
10 with the 'Turn-Up' a 5.

The non-dealer should keep either selection 16C or selection 16D. There is little to choose between them, both having five ways of forming 15/2 with the 'Turn-Up' card. On the basis of the better cards for pegging, the authors would choose selection 16C.

17A	A, A, 4, 4, 8	A, A, 8 (2)	10	17	0.98
		4, 4 (2)		6	0.34
17B	A, A, 4, 4, 8	4, 4, 8 (2)	16	13	0.98
		A, A (2)		2	0.17
17C	A, A, 4, 4, 8	A, A, 4 (2)	6	24	1.79
		4, 8 (0)		13	0.55
17D	A, A, 4, 4, 8	A, 4, 4 (2)	9	28	1.96
		A, 8 (0)		13	0.55

Comment: The dealer should choose selection 17A as it offers more chance of scoring by pegging as the cards are played.
The non-dealer should choose selection 17D rather than selection 17C as the former has more ways of forming 15/2 with the 'Turn-Up' card.

For selection 17C the ways are
(A + 4) with the 'Turn-Up' a '10' card, (twice)
(A + A + 4) with the 'Turn-Up' a 9

For selection 17D the ways are
(A + 4) with the 'Turn-Up' a '10' card, (twice)
(4 + 4) with the 'Turn-Up' a 7
(A + 4 + 4) with the 'Turn-Up' a 6.

(e) Two pairs are present and the 'Turn-Up' card might form a double sequence with either of the pairs and the other card in the hand

Advice to the dealer: *Keep the pair and the single card which offer the most ways of forming* 15/2 *with the 'Turn-Up' card and discard the other pair.*

Advice to the non-dealer: *Keep one pair and one card from the other pair and, of the two possible selections, choose that which offers the most ways of forming 15/2 with the 'Turn-Up' card. If the selections have the same number of ways, choose that with the better chance of scoring by pegging.*

Quiz: Assume, for each of the following examples, that the same set of cards was received by (a) the dealer and (b) the non-dealer. Which cards should be retained in hand? The answers to the quiz are given in the authors' comments in Table 7.7.

18. (4 + 4 + 6 + 8 + 8)	**20.** (7 + 7 + 9 + J + J)
19. (8 + 8 + 10 + Q + Q)	

Answers to the quiz

Table 7.7

Deals for which more than one selection gives the maximum score

(e) Two pairs present. The 'Turn-Up' card might form a double sequence with either of the pairs and the other card in the hand

Example	Cards Received	Selection for Hand and Discards	Numerical Sum of Selection for Hand	Number of Scoring 'Turn-Up' Cards	Weighted Average Increase in Score
18A	4, 4, 6, 8, 8	4, 4, 6 (2)	14	21	1.66
		8, 8 (2)		6	0.51
18B	4, 4, 6, 8, 8	6, 8, 8 (2)	22	17	1.66
		4, 4 (2)		6	0.34
18C	4, 4, 6, 8, 8	4, 4, 8 (2)	16	12	0.94
		6, 8 (0)		17	0.98
18D	4, 4, 6, 8, 8	4, 8, 8 (2)	20	12	0.94
		4, 6 (0)		13	0.81

Comment: The dealer should keep selection 18A where 15/2 can be formed if the 'Turn-Up' card is a 5 or a 7 rather than selection 18B where only a 7 will produce 15/2. Selections 18C and 18D both have four ways of forming 15/2 with the 'Turn-Up' card. Because the dealer is more likely to put a 7 rather than a 5 into the crib it is probably better for the non-dealer to choose selection 18D.

19A	8, 8, 10, Q, Q	8, 8, 10 (2)	26	17	1.32
		Q, Q (2)		6	0.51
19B	8, 8, 10, Q, Q	10, Q, Q (2)	30	13	1.32
		8, 8 (2)		6	0.51
19C	8, 8, 10, Q, Q	8, 8, Q (2)	26	12	0.77
		10, Q (0)		13	0.81
19D	8, 8, 10, Q, Q	8, Q, Q (2)	28	12	0.77
		8, 10 (0)		17	0.81

Comment: The dealer should choose either selection 19A or selection 19B. If the 'Turn-Up' card is a 5 or a Q the same number of points are gained from either of them. The choice between them is a gamble and depends on which cards are most likely to be discarded by the opponent. The dealer knows that the opponent will discard the best balking cards possible and, on that basis will choose a Q rather than a 7. However, the dealer also knows that while there are only two Q's amongst the 47 'unknown' cards there are four 7's. On that basis it is probably better to choose selection 19B.
Selections 19C and 19D both have three ways of forming 15/2 with the 'Turn-Up' card and there is little difference in the quality of the balking cards from them. It is difficult for the non-dealer to make a choice but, on balance, it is probably better to choose selection 19C.

20A	7, 7, 9, J, J	7, 7, 9 (2)	23	17	1.49
		J, J (2)		6	0.51
20B	7, 7, 9, J, J	9, J, J (2)	29	17	1.32
		7, 7 (2)		10	0.68
20C	7, 7, 9, J, J	7, 7, J (2)	24	18	0.94
		9, J (0)		17	0.8
20D	7, 7, 9, J, J	7, J, J (2)	27	12	0.77
		7, 9 (0)		13	0.81

Comment: For similar reasons to those stated in example 19, the dealer should choose selection 20B.
The non-dealer should choose selection 20C because it has four ways of forming 15/2 with the 'Turn-Up' card whereas selection 20D only has two.

For selection 20C the ways are:
7 with the 'Turn-Up' an 8 (twice)
J with the 'Turn-Up' a 5
(7 + 7) with the 'Turn-Up' an A

For selection 20D the ways are:
7 with the 'Turn-Up' an 8
J with the 'Turn-Up' a 5 (twice)

(f) Two pairs are present and the 'Turn-Up' card can form sequences with only one of the pairs and the other card in the hand

Advice to the dealer: *Discard the pair that cannot form sequences*

Advice to the non-dealer: *Keep one pair of cards and one card from the other pair choosing the best balking cards to the dealer's crib.*

Quiz: Which cards should be retained in hand by (a) the dealer and (b) the non-dealer?

21. (2 + 4 + 4 + Q + Q)	**22.** (2 + 2 + 8 + 8 + 10)

Answers to the quiz

Table 7.8 — Deals for which more than one selection gives the maximum score (f) Two pairs present — The 'Turn-Up' card can form sequences with only one of the pairs and the other card in the hand					
Example	**Cards Received**	**Selection for Hand and Discards**	**Numerical Sum of Selection for Hand**	**Number of Scoring 'Turn-Up' Cards**	**Weighted Average Increase in Score**
21A	2, 4, 4, Q, Q	2, 4, 4 (2)	10	21	1.49
		Q, Q (2)		6	0.51
21B	2, 4, 4, Q, Q	2, Q, Q (2)	22	13	0.98
		4, 4 (2)		6	0.34
21C	2, 4, 4, Q, Q	4, 4, Q (2)	18	16	0.94
		2, Q (0)		13	0.55
21D	2, 4, 4, Q, Q	4, Q, Q (2)	24	12	0.94
		2, 4 (0)		13	0.64
Comment: The dealer should keep selection 21A. The non-dealer should keep 21C so that the discards are as widely separated as possible.					
22A	2, 2, 8, 8, 10	8, 8, 10 (2)	26	17	1.32
		2, 2 (2)		6	0.34
22B	2, 2, 8, 8, 10	2, 2, 10 (2)	18	17	0.98
		8, 8 (2)		6	0.51
22C	2, 2, 8, 8, 10	2, 2, 8 (2)	16	12	0.94
		8, 10 (0)		17	0.81
22D	2, 2, 8, 8, 10	2, 8, 8 (2)	20	12	0.94
		2, 10 (0)		13	0.55
Comment: The dealer should keep selection 22A. The non-dealer should keep 22D so that the discards are as widely separated as possible.					

THERE IS NO SCORE FROM ANY OF THE POSSIBLE SELECTIONS

(g) An (A + 4) combination is present

Advice to the dealer: *Discard the* (A + 4) *combination because there is a better chance of the combination scoring in the crib than in the hand.*

Advice to the non-dealer: *Keep the selection containing the* (A + 4) *combination.*

Quiz: Which cards should be retained in hand by (a) the dealer and (b) the non-dealer?

23. (A + 3 + 4 + 6 + 7)	**24.** (A + 3 + 4 + 7 + 9)

Answers to the quiz

Table 7.9

Deals for which there is no score from any of the possible selections

(g) An (A + 4) combination is present

Example	Cards Received	Selection for Hand and Discards	Numerical Sum of Selection for Hand	Number of Scoring 'Turn-Up' Cards	Weighted Average Increase in Score
23A	A, 3, 4, 6, 7	A, 3, 4 (0)	8	40	1.96
		6, 7 (0)		22	1.28
23B	A, 3, 4, 6, 7	3, 6, 7 (0)	16	25	1.70
		A, 4 (0)		22	0.94
23C	A, 3, 4, 6, 7	A, 4, 6 (0)	11	37	1.96
		3, 7 (0)		14	0.6
Comment: The dealer should choose selection 23B and discard the (A + 4) combination and hope that the non-dealer will put at least one '10' card into the crib. The non-dealer should choose selection 23C which keeps the (A + 4) combination in the hand and gives better balking cards than from selection 23A.					
24A	A, 3, 4, 7, 9	A, 3, 4 (0)	8	40	1.96
		7, 9 (0)		14	0.85
24B	A, 3, 4, 7, 9	3, 7, 9 (0)	19	21	1.27
		A, 4 (0)		22	0.94
24C	A, 3, 4, 7, 9	A, 4, 9 (0)	14	37	1.7
		3, 7 (0)		14	0.6
Comment: For similar reasons to those given in example 23, the dealer should choose selection 24B and the non-dealer selection 24C.					

(h) Either a (6 + 7), or a (6 + 8) or a (7 + 9) combination is present

Advice to the dealer: *Discard the combination.*

Advice to the non-dealer: *Keep the combination.*

Quiz

Assume, for each of the following examples, that the same set of cards was received by (a) the dealer and (b) the non-dealer. Which cards should be retained in hand? The answers to the quiz are given in the authors' comments in Table 7.10.

25. (A + 6 + 7 + 10 + K)	**27.** (2 + 6 + 8 + J + K)
26. (3 + 6 + 7 + Q +K)	**28.** (A + 3 + 7 + 9 + K)

Answers to the quiz

Table 7.10

Deals for which there is no score from any of the possible selections

(h) Either a (6 + 7), a (6 + 8) or a (7 + 9) combination is present

Example	Cards Received	Selection for Hand and Discards	Numerical Sum of Selection for Hand	Number of Scoring 'Turn-Up' Cards	Weighted Average Increase in Score
25A	A, 6, 7, 10, K	A, 6, 7 (0)	14	25	1.83
		10, K (0)		10	0.60
25B	A, 6, 7, 10, K	A, 10, K (0)	21	17	1.06
		6, 7 (0)		22	1.28
Comment: The dealer should choose selection 25B and discard the (6 + 7) combination in the hope of a good score from the crib. The non-dealer should choose selection 25A and retain the combination.					
26A	3, 6, 7, Q, K	3, 6, 7 (0)	16	25	1.70
		Q, K (0)		14	0.85
26B	3, 6, 7, Q, K	3, Q, K (0)	23	21	1.32
		6, 7 (0)		22	1.28
26C	3, 6, 7, Q, K	6, 7, Q (0)	23	25	1.57
		3, K (0)		14	0.6
Comment: The dealer should choose selection 26B and discard the (6 + 7) combination. The non-dealer should retain the combination but should choose selection 26C rather than selection 26A, as 26C provides better balking cards to the crib.					

27A	2, 6, 8, J, K	2, 6, 8 (0)	16	25	1.49
		J, K (0)		14	0.85
27B	2, 6, 8, J, K	2, J, K (0)	22	21	1.32
		6, 8 (0)		18	1.02
27C	2, 6, 8, J, K	6, 8, J (0)	24	25	1.32
		2, K (0)		14	0.60
Comment: The dealer should choose selection 27B and discard the (6 + 8) combination. The non-dealer should retain the combination but should choose selection 27C rather than selection 27A, as 27C provides better balking cards to the crib.					
28A	A, 3, 7, 9, K	3, 7, 9 (0)	19	21	1.28
		A, K (0)		14	0.60
28B	A, 3, 7, 9, K	A, 3, K (0)	14	21	1.28
		7, 9 (0)		14	0.85
28C	A, 3, 7, 9, K	A, 7, 9 (0)	17	21	1.28
		3, K (0)		14	0.6
Comment: The dealer should choose selection 28B and discard the (7 + 9) combination. The non-dealer should retain the combination but should choose selection 28C rather than selection 28A, as 28C provides the better cards for pegging.					

(i) Three, four or all five of the cards received are separated by one rank and no two cards are of adjacent rank

Advice to the dealer

Keep the three cards separated by one rank which have the best chance of scoring 15/2 *with the 'Turn-Up' card and, if there is a choice in the selections, put cards into the crib which also have the best chance of scoring.*

Advice to the non-dealer

Keep the three cards separated by one rank which have the best chance of scoring 15/2 with the 'Turn-Up' card unless, by so doing, poor balking cards are given to the crib. In that case, the possibility of choosing another selection should be examined.

Quiz

Assume, for each of the following examples, that the same set of cards was received by (a) the dealer and (b) the non-dealer. Which cards should be retained in hand?

The answers to the quiz are given in the authors' comments in Table 7.11.

29. (2 + 4 + 6 + 8 + 10)	**31.** (2 + 6 + 8 + 10 + Q)
30. (3 + 7 + 9 + J + K)	

Answers to the quiz

Table 7.11					
Deals for which there is no score from any of the possible selections					
(i) Three or more cards are separated by one rank					
Example	**Cards Received**	**Selection for Hand and Discards**	**Numerical Sum of Selection for Hand**	**Number Of Scoring 'Turn-Up' Cards**	**Weighted Average Increase in Score**
29A	2, 4, 6, 8, 10	2, 4, 6 (0)	12	25	1.74
		8, 10 (0)		18	0.85
29B	2, 4, 6, 8, 10	4, 6, 8 (0)	18	29	1.74
		2, 10 (0)		14	0.60
29C	2, 4, 6, 8, 10	6, 8, 10 (0)	24	25	1.57
		2, 4 (0)		14	0.68

Comment: Selections 29A and 29B each have five ways of scoring 15/2 with the 'Turn-Up' card, whereas selection 29C has only four ways. The dealer should choose selection 29A as the discards are more likely to score in the crib and, conversely, the non-dealer should choose selection 29B.

For selection 29A the ways are:
6 with the 'Turn-Up' a 9
(2 + 4) with the 'Turn-Up' a 9
(2 + 6) with the 'Turn-Up' a 7
(4 + 6) with the 'Turn-Up' a 5
(2 + 4 + 6) with the 'Turn-Up' a 3

For selection 29B the ways are:
6 with the 'Turn-Up' a 9
8 with the 'Turn-Up' a 7
(4 + 6) with the 'Turn-Up' a 5
(4 + 8) with the 'Turn-Up' a 3
(6 + 8) with the 'Turn-Up' an A

For selection 29C the ways are:
6 with the 'Turn-Up' a 9
8 with the 'Turn-Up' a 7
10 with the 'Turn-Up' a 5
(6 + 8) with the 'Turn-Up' an A

30A	3, 7, 9, J, K	7, 9, J (0)	26	25	1.4
		3, K (0)		14	0.6
30B	3, 7, 9, J, K	9, J, K (0)	29	25	1.4
		3, 7 (0)		14	0.6
30C	3, 7, 9, J, K	3, J, K (0)	23	21	1.4
		7, 9 (0)		14	0.85

Comment: Selections 30A and 30B each have three ways of scoring 15/2 with the 'Turn-Up' card whereas selection 30C has four ways. In addition selection 30C provides the best discards to the crib and the dealer should choose this.
The non-dealer should choose 30A or 30B to avoid discarding the (7 + 9) combination.

For selection 30A the ways are:
7 with the 'Turn-Up' an 8
9 with the 'Turn-Up' a 6
J with the 'Turn-Up' a 5

For selection 30B the ways are:
9 with the 'Turn-Up' a 6
J and K with the 'Turn-Up' a 5

For selection 30C the ways are:
J with the 'Turn-Up' a 5
K with the 'Turn-Up' a 5
(3 + J) with the 'Turn-Up' a 2
(3 + K) with the 'Turn-Up' a 2

31A	2, 6, 8, 10, Q	6, 8, 10 (0)	24	25	1.57
		2, Q (0)		14	0.6
31B	2, 6, 8, 10, Q	8, 10, Q (0)	28	25	1.4
		2, 6 (0)		14	0.6
31C	2, 6, 8, 10, Q	2, 10, Q (0)	22	21	1.32
		6, 8 (0)		18	1.02

Comment: Selections 31A and 31B each have three ways of forming 15/2 with the 'Turn-Up' card whereas selection 31C has four ways and also provides the best discards to the crib. The dealer should choose selection 31C and, conversely, the non-dealer should choose either selection 31A or 31B. It doesn't matter which.

For selection 31A the ways are:
6 with the 'Turn-Up' a 9
8 with the 'Turn-Up' a 7
10 with the 'Turn-Up' a 5

For selection 31B the ways are:
8 with the 'Turn-Up' a 7
10 with the 'Turn-Up' a 5
Q with the 'Turn-Up' a 5

For selection 31C the ways are:
10 with the 'Turn-Up' a 5
Q with the 'Turn-Up' a 5
(2 + 10) with the 'Turn-Up' a 3
(2 + Q) with the 'Turn-Up' a 3

(j) None of the other options can be used

Advice to the dealer

Discard two cards of adjacent rank or separated by one rank.

Advice to the non-dealer

Discard two cards of widely differing rank.

A FLUSH CAN BE KEPT AS THE HAND

It is clear from the examples shown in Tables 7.1 to 7.11 that most three-card selections score less than three points. A flush guarantees a score of three and there is always the possibility of four points if the 'Turn-Up' card is of the same suit. Moreover, because all the cards in a flush are of different rank there is a better chance of scoring from the 'Turn-Up' card than when two cards of the same rank are retained as part of the hand. It therefore follows that, if all other possible selections from the cards received from the dealer score less than three points, the flush should be retained as the hand unless there is an overriding reason against that action. When there is another selection which scores three or more points a choice has to be made regarding the wisdom of retaining the flush as the hand.

The examples in Table 7.12 illustrate the extra considerations that are needed when it is possible to retain a flush and there are other selections which score three or more points. For the purpose of comparison the examples have been taken from Tables 7.1 and 7.5 and, for each example, a flush has been added as an extra selection. For those selections the three cards in the same suit have been indicated by means of asterisks. Selections in which four or all five cards are of the same suit have not been included but the same sort of considerations are necessary when these occur.

Quiz

Assume, for each of the following examples, that the same set of cards was received by (a) the dealer and (b) the non-dealer. Should the flush be retained as the hand? The answers to the quiz are given in the authors' comments in Table 7.12.

3. (3, 5*, 7*, 7, 8*)	**13.** (6*, 7*, 8, 9*, Q)
4. (2*, 3*, 8, 9*, 10)	**14.** (A*, 2, 3*, 4, 10*)
5. (2*, 3*, 5*, 10, K)	

Answers to the quiz

Table 7.12

Three of the cards received are of the same suit

Example	Cards Received	Selection for Hand and Discards	Numerical Sum of Selection for Hand	Number of Scoring 'Turn-Up' Cards	Weighted Average Increase in Score
3A	3, 5, 7,7, 8	7, 7, 8 (6)	22	17	1.83
		3, 5 (0)		28	1.28
3B	3, 5, 7, 7, 8	5, 7, 8 (2)	20	39	2.13
		3, 7 (0)		11	0.47
3C	3, 5*, 7*, 7, 8*	5*, 7*, 8* (5)	20	39	2.34
		3, 7 (0)		11	0.47

Comment: The dealer should ignore the flush, keep 3A and discard (3 + 5) to the crib. The non-dealer should keep the flush as the hand. There is a good chance that the point lost by not keeping selection 3A will be regained via the 'Turn-Up' card and the risk in discarding (3 + 5) is avoided.

Example	Cards Received	Selection for Hand and Discards	Numerical Sum of Selection for Hand	Number of Scoring 'Turn-Up' Cards	Weighted Average Increase in Score
4A	2, 3, 8, 9, 10	8, 9, 10 (3)	27	25	1.64
		2, 3 (0)		29	1.40
4B	2, 3, 8, 9, 10	2, 3, 10 (2)	15	33	1.96
		8, 9 (0)		17	1.04
4C	2*, 3*, 8, 9*, 10	2*, 3*, 9* (3)	14	36	2.38
		8, 10 (0)		17	0.79

Comment: The dealer should ignore the flush, keep selection 4A and discard (2 + 3) to the crib. In the final stages of the game, if the score from the crib is unlikely to be recorded, the dealer should keep 4C as it offers more chance of scoring by pegging. The non-dealer should keep the flush; the (2* + 3*) combination gives a good chance of an increase in the score due to the 'Turn-Up' card.

5A	2, 3, 5, 10, K	5, 10, K	(4)	25	17	1.23
		2, 3	(0)		28	1.36
5B	2, 3, 5, 10, K	2, 3, 5	(0)	10	39	2.64
		10, K	(0)		9	0.51
5C	2, 3, 5, 10, K	2, 3, 10	(2)	15	31	1.87
		5, K	(2)		17	0.98
5D	2*, 3*, 5*, 10, K	2*, 3*, 5*	(3)	10	39	2.85
		10, K	(0)		9	0.51

Comment: The dealer should keep selection 5C for the reasons given in Table 7.1. In the final stages of the game if neither the score from the hand nor from the crib is likely to be recorded, selection 5D may offer the best chance of scoring points by pegging as the cards are played.
The non-dealer should keep the flush (selection 5D). There is a good chance that the one point lost by not keeping selection 5A will be more than regained via the 'Turn-Up' card and having to discard a (2 + 3) combination is avoided.

13A	6, 7, 8, 9, Q	6, 7, 8	(5)	21	24	1.83
		9, Q	(0)		13	0.55
13B	6, 7, 8, 9, Q	7, 8, 9	(5)	24	16	1.49
		6, Q	(0)		13	0.55
13C	6*, 7*, 8, 9*, Q	6*, 7*, 9*	(5)	22	20	1.66
		8, Q	(0)		13	0.55

Comment: Both players should ignore the flush and keep selection 13A which offers the best chance of an increase in the score from the 'Turn-Up' card.

14A	A, 2, 3, 4, 10	A, 2, 3	(3)	6	31	1.83
		4, 10	(0)		13	0.55
14B	A, 2, 3, 4, 10	2, 3, 4	(3)	9	43	2.26
		A, 10	(0)		13	0.55
14C	A, 2, 3, 4, 10	2, 3, 10	(2)	15	31	1.83
		A, 4	(0)		21	0.89
14D	A, 2, 3, 4, 10	A, 4, 10	(2)	15	25	1.44
		2, 3	(0)		27	1.28
14E	A*, 2, 3*, 4, 10*	A*, 3*, 10*	(3)	14	19	1.34
		2, 4	(0)		13	0.62

Comment: The dealer should ignore the flush and keep selection 14D for the reasons given in Table 7.5. In the final stages of the game, if the score from the crib is unlikely to be recorded it is better to keep either selection 14A or selection 14B and hope to score points by pegging.
The non-dealer should keep selection 14B for the reasons given in Table 7.5

THE IMPORTANCE OF THE CRIB IN THE FIVE-CARD GAME

In the six-card game the dealer aims for the maximum score from the hand. As a secondary consideration, when there is more than one selection scoring the maximum without the aid of the 'Turn-Up' card, the dealer should choose the one with the best chance of scoring points in the crib. Obviously the non-dealer should try to balk the crib as much as possible. The situation is somewhat different in the five-card game where the crib is more valuable than the hand. More frequently than in the six-card game the dealer should discard either a 5, a (2 +3) or a (A + 4) combination, or another combination with a good chance of scoring in the crib even if, by doing so, the maximum score from the hand is not achieved. It is therefore useful for both players to have some knowledge of the most likely discards from the opponent and to use this knowledge when selecting the three cards to retain as the hand.

By examining, for a very large number of deals, the cards received by each player it has been possible to calculate the frequency of a card of each rank being discarded by either of the players. It should be remembered that discarding is a subjective process and that no two players will always discard in the same way. Therefore no set of frequencies relating to discarding should ever be taken as an absolute guide. However, the analysis of the results from the study does help the dealer to maximise, and the non-dealer to minimise, the score from the crib. The results of the analysis, expressed as percentage frequencies of cards being discarded to the crib, are shown in Table 7.13. Because of the inherent inaccuracies, and also for the sake of simplicity, the percentages have been rounded off to whole numbers. For easy comparison of the discards from the dealer and the non-dealer, the frequencies have been arranged in decreasing order of their occurrence. The analysis does not include any results which have been obtained from deals where the points obtained from pegging are more important than those from the hand and crib; that is, no results have been obtained from 'end-games'.

Table 7.13

Frequencies of Cards being Discarded to the Crib

% frequency	10	10	10	10	10	8	7	7	7	7	6	5	3
Dealer	Q	K	5	J	10	6	7	9	A	2	8	4	3
% frequency	11	11	11	10	9	9	8	8	6	6	6	5	0
Non-dealer	K	Q	2	9	10	J	A	7	8	6	4	3	5

Table 7.13 does not give any direct information relating to the frequency of either player choosing to discard certain pairs of cards such as (2 + 3), (A + 4), (6 + 8) and (7 + 9). Nevertheless, some helpful information can be deduced.

For example, although the dealer would like, whilst maintaining the maximum score from the cards received, to discard (2 +3) and (A + 4) combinations as often as possible it is difficult for him to do so. Since there is only a 3% probability of a 3 being discarded, there can, at the very best, only be a 3% probability that he is able to discard a (2 + 3) combination. The frequency of being able to discard an (A + 4) combination is slightly greater but is still very low. Furthermore, the dealer knows that any '10' cards discarded can only form 15/2 with the 'Turn-Up' card, as it is extremely unlikely for the non-dealer to discard a (2 + 3) or an (A + 4) combination. For the former combination the five cards received by the non-dealer would have to be (2 + 3 + 5 + 5 + 5) and for the latter the cards received would have to be (A + 4 + 5 + 5 + 5).

A number of points arise from the frequencies shown in Table 7.13:

1. Both players are most likely to discard '10' cards. There is no significant difference in the frequencies with which one '10' card, rather than another, will be discarded.
2. There is about a 40% frequency with which at least one '10' card will be discarded by both players.
3. Compared to the six-card game the dealer is able to discard a 5 with about twice the frequency. The non-dealer should therefore be aware that, if he discards a '10' card, there is twice the risk of the dealer scoring 15/2 from his crib.
4. Despite the risk of a 5 being amongst his opponent's discards, the non-dealer is frequently forced to discard a '10' card in order to obtain any score from his hand.
5. The non-dealer dare not risk discarding a 5, even though by keeping it as part of the hand, it does not score with either of the other two cards retained. Because of this he may have to risk putting better cards into the crib than he would have wished.
6. Mainly due to the inability of the non-dealer to discard a 5, there is no significant difference between the probabilities of discarding a 6, or a 7, or an 8 by either player. The dealer should take advantage of this, though he would be lucky if the non-dealer were forced to discard two of these cards.
7. The dealer should, whenever possible, take advantage of the fact the non-dealer is more likely to discard a 2 than a 3.

Summary of Advice on Scoring the Maximum Points in the Five-Card Game

It should be clear from the examples in Tables 7.1 to 7.12 that, in the five-card game, more thought is necessary when selecting the best discards for the maximum score from each deal than is usual in the six-card two-handed cribbage. In that game it is nearly always best to choose the selection which offers the maximum score without the aid of the 'Turn-Up' card and, if there is a choice of selections which gives this, to retain the selection with the cards having the lowest numerical sum.

This simple guidance applies to well over 99% of all the possible sets of cards which could be received from the dealer in the six-card game and simple flow charts to illustrate that guidance have been included in Chapter 6. Because of the more complex nature of the five-card game a large number of flow charts would be required to cover all of the eventualities and it is better, therefore, to select the discards using the guidance already given with the Tables. However, the summary below covers most of the advice given for the examples in those Tables.

In the summary the term 'maximum score' means, in the case of the dealer, the combined score, excluding the 'Turn-Up' card, of the points from the three cards retained as the hand *plus* any points from the two cards discarded to the crib without the help of the other discards. In the case of the non-dealer any points donated to the crib by his discards must be subtracted from those obtained from the hand in order to calculate the 'maximum score'.

Summary of the advice to the dealer

1. *Keep the selection with the maximum score unless there is another selection with a score differing from it by not more than 2 points which gives a better chance of a higher total score from the crib. If so, choose the other selection.*

2. *If there is more than one selection with the maximum score, keep the one which gives the best chance of a high score from the crib unless there is another selection, with a score differing by not more than 2 points from any of those with the maximum, which offers a better chance of a high total score from the crib. If so, keep the selection with the lower score.*

Summary of the advice to the non-dealer

1. *Keep the selection with the maximum score if, relative to any other selection, it scores 3 or more points. Do not keep the selection with the maximum score if there is another, differing by only 1 or 2 points from the selection with the maximum but which offers a much poorer chance of the dealer scoring from the crib. If so, keep the selection with the lower score. If the difference is greater than 2 points then keep the selection with the maximum score even if it is necessary to discard a 5.*

2. *If there is more than one selection with the maximum score choose the one with the greatest chance of balking the opponent's crib. But, if all the selections with the maximum score require poor balking cards to be discarded, and there is another selection with good balking discards which scores only one or two points less than the maximum score, choose the selection not giving the maximum score. If the difference is greater than 2 points choose one of the selections with the maximum score even if it is necessary to discard a 5.*

The examples in Table 7.14 have been included as further practice in choosing the best discards from those received at each deal. All of the examples show sets of cards which a player would feel very fortunate to receive, though unlikely to do so. They have been included because of the careful thought required when choosing the best way of discarding to the crib.

Quiz

Assume, for each of the following examples, that the same set of cards was received by (a) the dealer and (b) the non-dealer. Which cards should be retained in hand? The answers to the quiz are given in the authors' comments in Table 7.14.

32. (A + 2 + 2 + 3 + 3)	**38.** (4 + 5 + 7 + 7 + 8)
33. (5 + 5 + 10 + J + Q)	**39.** (4 + 5 + 6 + 7 + 8)
34. (5 + 5 + 5 + 10 + Q)	**40.** (2 + 5 + 6 + 6 + 9)
35. (4 + 5 + 5 + 5 + 6)	**41.** (2 + 3* + 6* + 7* + 8*)
36. (5 + 5 + J + J + J)	**42.** (3 + 5* + 6* + 7* + 8*)
37. (6 + 7 + 7 + 8 + 8)	

Answers to the quiz

Table 7.14

Potentially high scoring hands

Example	Cards Received	Selection for Hand and Discards	Numerical Sum of Selection for Hand	Number of Scoring 'Turn-Up' Cards	Weighted Average Increase in Score
32A	A, 2, 2, 3, 3	A, 2, 3 (3)	6	31	1.68
		2, 3 (0)		27	1.30
32B	A, 2, 2, 3, 3	A, 2, 2 (2)	5	23	1.23
		3, 3 (2)		6	0.34
32C	A, 2, 2, 3, 3	A, 3, 3 (2)	7	15	0.89
		2, 2 (2)		2	0.17
32D	A, 2, 2, 3, 3	2, 2, 3 (2)	7	31	2.68
		A, 3 (0)		7	0.34

Comment: The dealer should choose neither selection 32B nor selection 32C, which score the maximum points, but should choose selection 32A, even though the guaranteed score is one point less, and discard the (2 + 3) combination to the crib. The non-dealer should choose selection 32D.

33A	5, 5, 10, J, Q	10, J, Q (3)	30	19	1.38
		5, 5 (2)		15	1.36
33B	5, 5, 10, J, Q	5, 5, J (6)	20	15	1.57
		10, Q (0)		11	0.62

Comment: The dealer should choose selection 33A which, although not scoring the maximum, allows two 5's to be discarded to the crib which should more than recover the point lost by rejecting selection 33B.
The non-dealer should choose selection 33B.

34A	5, 5, 5, 10, Q	5, 5, 5 (8)	15	15	2.04
		10, Q (0)		11	0.60
34B	5, 5, 5, 10, Q	5, 5, 10 (6)	20	15	1.45
		5, Q (2)		15	0.81

Comment: The dealer should choose 34B because it offers the chance of a good score from the crib. If in the final stages of a game the only chance of winning is to make a very large score, it would be better to keep 34A and hope, despite the odds, that the 'Turn-Up' card was the fourth 5 which would take the score from the hand to 20 points.
The non-dealer should choose selection 34A.

35A	4, 5, 5, 5, 6	5, 5, 5 (8)	15	17	2.30
		4, 6 (0)		11	0.53
35B	4, 5, 5, 5, 6	4, 5, 6 (5)	15	35	2.07
		5, 5 (2)		17	1.49

Comment: The dealer should choose selection 35B because there is a good chance that the point lost from the maximum will be more than regained from the crib.
The non-dealer should choose selection 35A.

36A	5, 5, J, J, J	5, 5, J (6)	20	15	1.49
		J, J (2)		3	0.26
36B	5, 5, J, J, J	5, J, J (6)	25	15	0.89
		5, J (2)		15	0.77
36C	5, 5, J, J, J	J, J, J (6)	30	3	0.38
		5, 5 (2)		15	1.36

Comment: The dealer should choose selection 36C and hope that at least one '10' card is amongst the opponent's discards and the 'Turn-Up' card.
The non-dealer should choose 36A which avoids having to discard a 5 to the crib.

37A	6, 7, 7, 8, 8	6, 7, 8 (5)	21	23	1.60
		7, 8 (2)		11	0.79
37B	6, 7, 7, 8, 8	7, 7, 8 (6)	22	15	1.57
		6, 8 (0)		15	0.77

Comment: The dealer should choose selection 37A with a guaranteed score of 7 points from the hand and the crib.
The non-dealer should choose selection 37B because to choose selection 37A gives a net score of only 3 points.

38A	4, 5, 7, 7, 8	7, 7, 8 (6)	22	17	1.83
		4, 5 (0)		30	1.62
38B	4, 5, 7, 7, 8	5, 7, 8 (2)	20	40	2.17
		4, 7 (0)		8	0.47
38C	4, 5, 7, 7, 8	5, 7, 7 (2)	19	36	2.26
		4, 8 (0)		12	0.51

Comment: The dealer should choose selection 38A which gives the maximum score and allows a 5 to be discarded to the crib.
The non-dealer should also choose selection 38A and hope that, because of the 5 discarded, the score from the crib does not exceed the 4 points which would be lost by making any other selection.

39A	4, 5, 6, 7, 8	4, 5, 6 (5)	15	36	2.34
		7, 8 (2)		13	0.96
39B	4, 5, 6, 7, 8	6, 7, 8 (5)	21	24	1.87
		4, 5 (0)		29	1.51
39C	4, 5, 6, 7, 8	5, 6, 7 (3)	18	43	2.53
		4, 8 (0)		13	0.55

Comment: The dealer should choose selection 39B and hope that the 5 put in to the crib will more than compensate for the 2 points lost by not choosing selection 39A.
The non-dealer should choose selection 39C with the best balking cards. While it scores the same as selection 39A, it avoids having to discard a 5 and differs by only 2 points from selection 39B.

40A	2, 5, 6, 6, 9	6, 6, 9 (6)	21	9	0.81
		2, 5 (0)		26	1.11
40B	2, 5, 6, 6, 9	5, 6, 9 (2)	20	36	2.08
		2, 6 (0)		12	0.51
40C	2, 5, 6, 6, 9	5, 6, 6 (2)	17	36	2.77
		2, 9 (0)		12	0.51

Comment: Both players should choose selection 40A for reasons similar to those given in the comments for example 38.

41A	2, 3*, 6*, 7*, 8*	6*, 7*, 8* (8)	21	24	2.04
		2, 3* (0)		30	1.45
41B	2, 3*, 6*, 7*, 8*	3*, 7*, 8* (5)	18	24	1.62
		2, 6* (0)		13	0.55
Comment: Both players should choose selection 41A, the non-dealer hoping that by discarding the (2 + 3) combination the score from the crib does not exceed the difference of 3 points between selections 41A and 41B.					
42A	3, 5*, 6*, 7*, 8*	6*, 7*, 8* (8)	21	24	2.06
		3, 5* (0)		29	1.32
42B	3, 5*, 6*, 7*, 8*	5*, 6*, 7* (6)	18	43	2.74
		3, 8* (0)		13	0.55
Comment: The dealer should choose selection 42A. The non-dealer should choose selection 42B as there is only a 2 points difference between the selections and choosing 42B avoids having to discard a 5 to the crib.					

Chapter 8

SCORING BY PEGGING

In the previous chapters most of the emphasis has been placed on gaining the maximum score from the hand and the crib. For much of the game the discards are generally chosen with that in mind and the points by pegging are gained by the skill, and luck, of the players using cards which were not specifically selected to score by pegging.

This chapter gives guidance on the best way gaining points by pegging and of preventing the opponent gaining points by this means. The advice on playing the cards applies throughout the whole game even when the selection was biased towards the score from the hand. However, towards the end of a game, a player may be in a position when he feels that the only chance of winning is from the points scored as the cards are played and, when this is the case, he should discard with this in mind.

The non-dealer is always the first to lead and, in the five-card game, is the only one to do so as no further cards are played after the first 'Go' or '31' is reached even when some cards remain. In the six-card game all the cards from the hands must be played and the second lead, if there is one, belongs to the player who did not play the last card of the previous sum. Because of the cards already played the choice for the second lead is much reduced. In an earlier chapter general guidance was given about scoring by pegging. This chapter is included in order to take the argument further and to try to develop the skills required to ensure that the points from pegging are the maximum possible.

Advice on the leads and the replies

The following comments point out the advantages, and disadvantages, of leading with cards of different rank and include suggestions for the best replies to those leads. Obviously to follow one piece of advice often makes it impossible to follow another. This apparent paradox arises because it may be advantageous for a card of a particular rank to be used at different times during the count to '31', and a player has to choose the most opportune time to play that card.

The examples in the text and in the Tables illustrate this. For the sake of clarity the cards played by the dealer have asterisks. The scores obtained during the count are shown in round brackets and, if obtained by the dealer, are also highlighted with asterisks. Square brackets are used to enclose all the cards that have been played in full counts to 'Go' or '31'.

The comments on the lead are divided into two sections. The first deals with hands where the lead and the second card played from it, in conjunction with that played by the opponent, are unlikely to enable the leader to score by making either 15/2 or a sequence, and where any points gained will probably arise by pairing cards and by taking the count to 'Go' or '31'. These are regarded as defensive leads and aim to restrict the points gained by the opponent.

The second section deals with leads from hands containing groups of cards, such as (A + 4), (7 + 8) and (5 + 6 + 7), where the first lead can have a marked effect on the order in which the remaining cards should be played. These are attacking leads even though the lead may have been chosen to minimise the risk of points being scored by the opponent throughout the whole of the count. It should always be remembered that the opponent, when replying, has no knowledge of the cards in the leader's hand and should assume that all first leads are attacking.

A. DEFENSIVE LEADS (Hands that do not contain important groupings of cards)

1. The lead is a 5

Do not do this. There is a high probability that the dealer holds at least one '10' card and can, therefore, score 15/2 by playing it.

2. The lead is a low card, either a 4, a 3, a 2 or an A

The dealer cannot reply with a card to make 15/2 and can score only by pairing the lead. These low cards are therefore regarded as 'safe' leads. Although both an A or a 2 are 'safe' first leads they frequently score points by completing the count at 'Go' and '31' and it is generally wise to retain them with the hope of scoring at the end of the count.

The possible replies from the dealer are as follows:

(a) Pairing the lead

The dealer should be cautious about doing this because the non-dealer may have led from a pair hoping to score 6 points for 'pairs royal'. The relative positions on the board are useful as a guide when deciding on the wisdom of pairing the lead. Whenever possible the dealer should reply to the initial lead and make 15/2.

With the most points on the board or with a hand so poor that the only points expected are from pegging, the dealer should pair the lead. In the final stages of the game, if the only chance of winning is by taking every opportunity of scoring, the dealer should similarly take the risk of his opponent scoring 'pairs royal' and should pair the lead. Otherwise the dealer should avoid doing so.

(b) Playing a '10' card

The initial lead may have come from either a (2 + 3) or an (A + 4) combination. If a '10' card is then played the non-dealer can score 15/2 by playing the other half of the combination. However, playing a '10' card is often unavoidable and even if it is not it may be the safest reply possible.

(c) Playing a 9

This is a 'safe' reply to follow a lead of a 4, a 2 or an A as the non-dealer can score only by playing another 9 for a pair or by making 15/2 with the other low card from either a (4 + 2) or a (A + 5) combination. However, it is less 'safe' as a reply to follow a lead of a 3. The non-dealer may have led from a pair of 3's and would then be able to reply with the other one and score 2 points for making 15/2. It is generally thought to be more likely that the non-dealer will have selected a hand containing a pair of 3's than to have kept a (2 + 4) combination.

Similarly the first lead would probably be one of the other cards in the hand if the hand contained an (A + 5) combination. It is usually more attractive for the non-dealer to hold back the A in the hope that it would make 'Go' or '31'.

(d) Playing an 8

This is a 'safe' reply as the non-dealer can score only by either pairing it or by having the appropriate low card to make 15/2.

(e) Playing a 7

This is a 'safe' reply to follow a lead of either a 3 or a 2 as the non-dealer can score only by playing another 7 or by making 15/2. It is less 'safe' to follow a lead of a 4 in case the non-dealer has led from a pair of them. It is dangerous to play a 7 to follow a lead of an A because, by playing another 7, the non-dealer can score 4 points, 2 for a pair and 2 for making 15/2.

(f) Playing a 6

This is a 'safe' reply to follow a lead of a 2 or an A as the non-dealer can score, with safety, only by playing another 6 to score 2 for a pair. It would be dangerous for the non-dealer to make 15/2 by playing either a 7, [2, 6*, 7 (2)] or an 8, [A, 6*, 8 (2)], because of the risk of the dealer being able to score with a sequence, cards being played in the order [2, 6*, 7 (2), 8* (3*)] or [A, 6*, 8 (2), 7* (3*)]. It is dangerous for the dealer to use a 6 as the reply to a lead of a 3 in case the non-dealer has another 6 and can score 4 points, 2 for a pair and 2 for making 15/2.

A 6 is also not a safe reply following a lead of 4; there is the risk of giving away 5 points if the non-dealer plays a 5 to score 3 points for a sequence and 2 more for 15/2, i.e., [4, 6*, 5 (3 + 2)]. Whenever possible it is wise for either player to 'play away', that is, avoid playing a card of adjacent rank, or separated by one rank, from the previous card played.

(g) Playing a 5

This is a 'safe' reply to follow a 2 or an A as the non-dealer can score only by playing either another 5 or with the appropriate card to make 15/2. With a lead of either a 3 or a 4 the dealer should 'play away'; to reply with a 5 gives the non-dealer the chance to score with a sequence and possibly with 15/2 as well, i.e., [3, 5*, 4 (3)] and [4, 5*, 6 (3 + 2)].

In the five-card game, with only one count to 'Go', there is only one chance of forming 15/2 with a '10' card, should that be the lead of the non-dealer. In the six-card game and in three- and four-handed cribbage, when there are usually two or more counts to 'Go', it is often wise to delay playing a 5 in the hope that it will combine later with a '10' card to make 15/2. Therefore, if the first lead is a low card, do not reply with a 5 but, if possible, choose a more suitable card.

3. The non-dealer leads a 6

The dealer can score only by pairing the lead or by making 15/2 by playing a 9. If the hand contains neither a 6 nor a 9 the dealer should reply with a '10' card if possible. If none of these options is possible, try to 'play away' and not reply with either a 4, 5, 7 or 8 because of the risk of the non-dealer scoring 3 points for a sequence and possibly 2 points for 15/2 as well, e.g., [6, 4*, 5 (3 + 2)]. However, it is safe for the dealer to reply with either a 7 or an 8 if his hand also contains either a 9 or a '10' card. If the non-dealer plays an 8 next to claim a sequence, the count becomes '21'. The dealer's '10' card can make '31' or his 9 score 4 points for another sequence and probably a further point for 'Go' e.g., [6, 7*, 8 (3), '10*' (2*)] and [6, 7*, 8 (3), 9* (4* + 1*)] or [6, 8*, 7 (3), '10*' (2*)] and [6, 8*,7 (3),9* (4* + 1*)]. Furthermore the dealer should try not to reply with a 3 because the non-dealer may have led from a pair of 6's, i.e., [6, 3*, 6 (2)].

4. The non-dealer leads a 7

The dealer should consider carefully before playing an 8 to make 15/2. The non-dealer may have led from either a (6 + 7) or a (7 + 9) combination and, following the dealer's reply, could form a sequence e.g., [7, 8* (2*), 6 (3)] or [7, 8* (2*), 9 (3)]. It becomes more attractive for the dealer to play an 8 if the hand also contains a 6 and a 9, so that the non-dealer's 3-card sequence can be converted into a 4-card one.

If, after a lead of 7, the dealer replies with an 8 to make 15/2, the non-dealer can safely play a 6 and score 3 points for a sequence, even though the count is taken to '21', as long as the hand also contains an A. If the dealer then plays a '10' card for '31' the non-dealer is one point ahead *in the final stages of the count*, i.e., [7, 8* (2*), *6 (3), '10*' (2*)*]. The dealer is also a point ahead *in the final stages* if the dealer plays a 9 for a 4-card sequence because the non-dealer's A will take the count to '31'. i.e., [7, 8* (2*), *6 (3), 9* (4*), A (2)*].

5. The non-dealer leads either an 8 or a 9

Both are fairly safe leads. When the hand contains these cards with others of adjacent rank, careful consideration should be given to which should be used as the first lead so that the maximum number of points can be obtained. This is discussed later. The dealer should reply by scoring 15/2 if possible; otherwise pair the lead or 'play away'.

6. The non-dealer leads a '10' card

This is not recommended in case the dealer holds a 5. Nevertheless, the non-dealer is sometimes forced to do so if the hand contains only 5's and '10' cards. With two or more '10' cards the non-dealer should lead from a pair, if held, or a '10' card of adjacent rank to, or separated by one rank from another. When forced to lead from a (10 + K) combination, the K should be led as there is less chance of it being paired by the dealer who is more likely to have retained a 10 rather a K when discarding to the crib. The dealer should reply with a 5 if possible; otherwise pair the lead or 'play away'.

B. ATTACKING LEADS (Hands that do contain important groupings of cards)

1. Leading from a pair of cards of the same rank

For the first lead in the six-card game it is generally better to avoid doing this unless the rank of the pair is 8 or greater. The opponent will be wary of pairing the lead because of the danger of losing 6 points for 'pairs royal'. When the pair is of low rank it often pays to delay playing one of them in the hope that the opponent will be less cautious or cannot avoid pairing it. On the other hand, if the pair is of high rank, e.g., '10' cards, it is best to use one of them as the lead as this may be the only chance of obtaining 'pairs royal'. The same arguments apply to the dealer; do not reply with a card from a pair but try to keep it until there may be a better chance of scoring for 'pairs royal'. If, in the final stages of a game the dealer is well behind and can only win with the points pegged, the lead should be paired in the hope that 12 points for 'double pairs royal' can be recorded e.g., [7, 7* (2*), 7 (6), 7* (12*)].

The situation is different in the five-card game. With only one count to 'Go' there will generally be only one opportunity of scoring for 'pairs royal' and so, with the exception of pairs of A's, 2's, and 5's, the first lead from the hand should be from the pair. It is wise to keep low cards to use at the end of the count and a 5 should never be led. With a pair of 7's it is sensible to lead one and to aim for 'pairs royal', even though the count would be taken to 21, because this gains more points than with a different lead.

2. Leading from an (A + 4) combination

Lead the 4 rather than the A. The latter is generally more useful than the 4 for reaching 'Go' or '31' if the dealer has not played a '10' card and allowed the A to make 15/2.

3. Leading from a (2 + 3) combination

Lead the 3 rather than the 2 for similar reasons to those described above.

4. Leading from a (6 + 9) combination

Lead the 6 rather than the 9. If the dealer then replies with a 9 to make 15/2 it is safe to play the 9 from the combination to score 2 for a pair. The dealer's hand would have to contain one of the four 7's in the pack to make '31', i.e., [6, 9* (2*), 9 (2), 7* (2*)].

The converse does not hold. If the 9 is led, and the dealer replies with a 6, it is not safe to score 2 for a pair by playing the 6 from the combination; the running total would be '21' and the dealer could score '31' by playing any of the sixteen '10' cards from the pack, i.e., [9, 6* (2*), 6 (2), Q* (2*)].

5. Leading from a (7 + 8) combination

Try not to do this but, if there is no alternative, lead the 8 rather than the 7. In either case, if the non-dealer is forced to play the second card from the combination after the dealer's reply to score 15/2, there is the risk of losing 'pairs royal'.

With the 8 as the lead, the total count is taken to 'Go' with the loss of 7 points, whereas a lead of the 7, and 'pairs royal' with three 8's, takes the count to '31' with the loss of 8 points, i.e., either [8, 7* (2*), 7 (2),7* (6* + 1*)] or [7, 8* (2*), 8 (2), 8* (6* + 2*)].

6. Leading from a (6 + 7 + 8) combination

In six-card cribbage do not lead a card from the combination. Use the fourth card from the hand unless it is a 5. The decision regarding the best lead is more complicated in five-card cribbage, as the hand contains only three cards, or for the dealer's lead at the start of the second count in the six-card game if the cards played in the first have been ['10', '10*' (2*), '10' (6 + 1)].

It is necessary to plan, in relation to the initial lead and the possible replies, which of the other two cards from the combination should be played second to try to recoup some, or all, of the points lost by the first reply. In selecting the lead it is wise to assume the worst possible scenario, i.e., that the reply will always score 2 points, either by pairing the lead or by making 15/2.

(a) The first lead is the 6

Do not do this. If the opponent pairs the lead no points can be scored by playing either the 7 or the 8 from the combination; moreover the other player can then score again by making either another pair or a sequence, i.e., [6, 6* (2*), 7, 7* (2*)] and [6, 6* (2*), 7, 8* (3*)] or [6, 6* (2*), 8, 8* (2*)] and [6, 6* (2*), 8, 7* (3*)].

Similar problems occur when the opponent replies with a 9 to make 15/2. Neither the 7 nor the 8 from the combination can be played with safety, i.e., [6, 9* (2*), 7, 7* (2*)] and [6, 9* (2*), 7, 8* (3*)] or [6, 9* (2*), 8, 8* (2* + 2*)] and [6, 9* (2*), 8, 7* (3*)].

(b) The first lead is either the 7 or the 8

If the reply is another 7 or 8 to make 15/2 the second card from the combination must score, either 3 points for a sequence or 2 points for a pair. The risk of the opponent scoring further points with the fourth card played cannot be avoided, e.g., [7, 8* (2*), 6 (3), '10' *(2*)], [7, 8* (2*), 6 (3), 9* (4*)], [7, 8* (2*), 8 (2), 8* (8*)] etc.

Similar scoring patterns follow if the 8 from the combination is used as the initial lead. Despite the risk of losing 6 points for 'pairs royal' and a further 2 points for '31' it is better, unless the position in the game is critical and the extra point is required, to pair the reply than to make a sequence. There is only about a 4% chance that the opponent can score the 8 points for 'pairs royal' and '31' and, if any other card completes the count, only 1 point is lost for 'Go'.

7. Leading from a (7 + 8 + 9) combination

In six-card cribbage avoid leading from the combination. Play the other card unless it is a 5.

In the five-card game, and for the second count in the six-card game if the cards played in the first have been ['10', '10*' (2*), '10' (6 + 1)], the lead should either be the 7 or the 8. The reasons are similar to those for the (6 + 7 + 8) combination. If the opponent responds to the lead of either the 7 or the 8 to make 15/2, the reply can either be paired or the 9 played to score 3 points for a sequence. In so doing there is always the risk that the opponent can play a card to score either 'pairs royal' or another sequence, e.g., [7, 8* (2), 8 (2), 8* (6* + 2*)] and [7, 8* (2*), 9 (3), 6* (4* + 1*)], etc. Whether to pair the reply or make a sequence depends on the positions in the game held at that time but it is generally better to pair the reply.

The 9 is the worst possible lead from the combination. If the opponent replies with a 6 to make 15/2, neither the 7 nor the 8 from the combination will score points for the third card played. In addition the 7 or the 8 next leaves the way open for a high score from the fourth card played, e.g., [9, 6* (2*), 8, 7* (4* + 1*)] or [9, 6* (2*), 7, 8* (4* + 1*)].

8. Leading from (6 + 6 + 7 + 8), (6 + 7 + 7 + 8) and (6 + 7 + 8 + 8) combinations

A 6 is the worst possible lead from any of these. If the reply is a 9 for 15/2, no score can be made with any of the other cards from the combination. Always try to lead so that there is the greatest chance of scoring from the third card and the least from the fourth card played in the count to 'Go'. Thus from (6 + 6 + 7 + 8) lead either the 7 or the 8 so that the reply can be paired if the opponent makes 15/2, e.g., [7, 8* (2*), 8 (2)] etc. or [8, 7* (2*),7 (2)] etc.

From (6 + 7 + 7 + 8) lead the 8 because, if the opponent plays a 7 to make 15/2, one of the 7's from the combination can be played with relative safety. Because a third 7 is held in the hand there is only about a 2% chance that the opponent has the fourth and can play it to score 6 points for 'pairs royal' and one for 'Go', e.g., [8, 7* (2*), 7 (2), 7* (6* + 1*)].

It is riskier to lead one of the 7's because, if the opponent plays an 8 for 15/2, the only safe reply is the other 7 for no score. To reply with the 6, and to score 3 points for a sequence, takes the count to 21 and, as described above, gives the opponent the chance of scoring with a '10' card for 2 points, or a 9*, a 7* or a 5* for another sequence and 4 points, or with another 6 for 2 points, e.g., [7, 8* (2*), 6 (3), '10*' (2*)] or [7, 8* (2*), 6 (3), 9* (4* + 1*)] or [7, 8* (2*), 6 (3), 6* (2*)].

It is also not safe, having led a 7, to pair the opponent's reply if he plays an 8 for 15/2. There is the danger of losing 6 points for 'pairs royal' and 2 more for taking the count to '31', e.g., [7, 8* (2*), 8 (2), 8* (6* + 2*)]. Holding (6 + 7 + 7 + 8) in hand there is twice the chance that the opponent will hold a pair of 8's than a pair of 7's.

For similar reasons the 7 should be led from the (6 + 7 + 8 + 8) combination. These comments emphasise that with both the (6 + 7 + 7 + 8) and (6 + 7 + 8 + 8) combinations more points are likely to be lost if the lead is made from the pair of 7's or 8's even though the opponent's reply at 15/2 can be countered with a sequence. There is a good chance that the dealer can score by making another sequence and 'Go' or '31'.

9. Leading from (7 + 7 + 8 + 9), (7 + 8 + 8 + 9) and (7 + 8 + 9 + 9) combinations

For similar reasons to those earlier, do not lead a 9 from any of these combinations in case the opponent replies with a 6 to make 15/2. No points can be pegged with any of the cards remaining in the hand. There is also considerable risk that when the 7 or the 8 is played as the next card the dealer will be able to form a sequence, e.g., [9, 6* (2*), 7, 8* (4* + 1*)]. It therefore pays to follow the same rules as those given above and to lead an 8 so that, if the dealer replies with a 7 for 15/2, a 9 can be played with safety for a sequence.

In very unusual circumstances it can pay to lead a 9. For example, if in the final stages of a game the non-dealer's hand is (7 + 8 + 9 + 9) and despite this the chances of winning are small, consider leading one of the 9's in the hope of gaining 6 points for 'pairs royal'.

10. Leading from (9 + 10 + J), (10 + J + Q) and (J + Q + K) combinations

From (9 + 10 + J) and (J + Q + K), lead the card from the centre of the combination in case the opponent is forced to reply with a card of close rank to that led. One of the other '10' cards can then be played to make a sequence and, very probably, 'Go' as well. This advice is also true for the (10 + J + Q) combination, but note the increased risk of the J being paired because the dealer is more likely to retain a J rather than any other '10' card.

11. Leading from hands containing four '10' cards

If all the cards are of different rank lead the Q, rather than the J, so that a sequence can be scored if the opponent replies with either a K, J or 10. As the Q is a more attractive discard than a J there is less likelihood of the Q lead being paired. If two of the four cards are of the same rank, lead one of them. If two pairs are present, and one or both of the pairs are Q's or K's, lead from the higher rank because the opponent is more likely to have discarded a Q or a K.

12. Leading from combinations of low cards in sequence

(a) All the cards in the hand form a single sequence

In general, lead a middle card from a sequence, but not if it is a 5. For example, in five-card cribbage, lead the 4 from (3 + 4 + 5) and (4 + 5 + 6) so that a sequence can be pegged if the opponent cannot 'play away' from the card led. In the six-card game lead the 3 from hands such as (A + 2 + 3 + 4) and (2 + 3 + 4 + 5) so that 15/2 can be scored if the reply is a '10' card or a sequence formed if the opponent cannot 'play away'. Avoid leading a 6 or 7, which could allow the opponent to score 15/2 with the reply. At first sight leading the 4 from (4 + 5 + 6 + 7) appears to reduce the chance of forming a sequence, but the opponent would not reply with either a 5 or a 6 unless forced to do so (because the hand only contains 5's and 6's, a rarity).

(b) One of the cards in a three-card sequence is paired

Lead to give the greatest chance of scoring from the third card and the least from the fourth card played. The lead should be the central card from the pair of sequences provided that this does not mean that a 5 has to be led. For example, from (A + A + 2 + 3), (A + 2 + 2 + 3) and (A + 2 + 3 + 3) the lead should be a 2, which allows the A's to be kept until later in the hope of using them to score for 'Go' or '31'.

For (2 + 2 + 3 + 4), (2 + 3 + 3 + 4) and (2 + 3 + 4 + 4) it is best to lead a 3.

For (3 + 3 + 4 + 5), (3 + 4 + 4 + 5) and (3 + 4 + 5 + 5) it is best to lead a 4.

For (4 + 4 + 5 + 6), (4 + 5 + 5 + 6) and (4 + 5 + 6 + 6) it is also best to lead a 4.

Examples to illustrate card play during pegging

The examples in Tables 8.1 and 8.2 are the same as those used in the Tables in Chapters 6 and 7. For each example the selections chosen in those chapters have been used to illustrate the advice given in the text of this Chapter.

The selections from the examples with odd numbers have been allocated to the non-dealer and those with even numbers to the dealer. For both the six-card and the five-card games the examples with consecutive numbers play against each other.

Quiz

Six-Card Game

For each of the following pairs of hands with consecutive numbers decide how to play the cards during pegging. Remember that the first lead belongs to the non-dealer and that all the cards must be played.

The advice given in the text covers the general aspects of pegging. Remember that a player should not adopt a set of rules blindly but should vary the tactics depending on the total number of points relative to the opponent's score and how near the game is to completion.

The answers to the quiz are given in the authors' comments in Table 8.1 but note that they are more subjective than those given in the other Tables.

#	Non-dealer	Dealer	#	#	Non-dealer	Dealer	#
1	6, 7, 8, 9	2*, 2*, 5*, 8*	2	3	A, 4, 10, Q	2*, 3*, J*, K*	4
5	6, 7, 8, 8	6*, 6*, 8*, 9*	6	7	2, 4, 6, 8	4*, 6*, 8*, 10*	8
9	A, 3, 4, 10	2*, 4*, 6*, 7*	10	11	2, 2, 4, 4	8*, 9*, 10*, J*	12
13	2, 3, 10, J	4*, 5*, 6*, 9*	14	15	3, 4, 5, 6	3*, 4*, 5*, 6*	16
17	8, 9, 10, 10	6*, 7*, 7*, 8*	18	19	7, 7, 8, 9	4*, 4*, 5*, 6*	20
21	6, 7, 8, 8	A*, A*, 2*, 3*	22	23	A, A, 2, 3	2*, 2*, 3*, 4*	24
25	A, 2, 3, 3	2*, 2*, 3*, 3*	26				

Answers to quiz *Scoring by pegging, six-card cribbage*

Notes: The same examples are used as in Tables 6.2 to 6.7. The non-dealer has been given the examples with odd numbers and the dealer those with even and the first selection of each example has been used. The scores are shown in brackets. The cards and scores of the dealer have asterisks. The comments are based on how the authors would play these hands. Remember that neither player would have any knowledge of the cards in the other's hand.

<table>
<tr><th colspan="5">Table 8.1 — Scoring by pegging
Six-card cribbage</th></tr>
<tr><th>#</th><th>Non-dealer</th><th>Cards played and points gained</th><th>Dealer</th><th>#</th></tr>
<tr><td>1</td><td>6, 7, 8, 9</td><td>7, 8* (2*), 9 (3), 5*, 2* (2*)
8, 2*, 6 (1)</td><td>2*, 2*, 5*, 8*</td><td>2</td></tr>
<tr><td colspan="5">Comment: The safest lead is the 7, because if the dealer replies with an 8*, then the 6 or the 9 will score for a sequence. It is better to play the 9 and to avoid taking the score to '21'. By playing the 5* as second card the dealer takes the count as close to '31' as possible and gives the opponent the minimal chance of playing a card.</td></tr>
<tr><td>3</td><td>A, 4, 10, Q</td><td>4, K*, A (2), J*, 3*, 2* (1*)
10, Q (1)</td><td>2*, 3*, J*, K*</td><td>4</td></tr>
<tr><td colspan="5">Comment: Despite the risk that the non-dealer may have led from an (A + 4) combination, the dealer should 'play away' and reply with one of his '10*' cards, preferably the K, because the non-dealer is more likely to have discarded a K than a J. There is, therefore, less risk of losing '2 for a pair'. It is dangerous for the dealer to reply with either his 2* or his 3* in case the non-dealer's hand contains other low cards which could combine to form a sequence.</td></tr>
<tr><td>5</td><td>6, 7, 8, 8</td><td>7, 8*(2*), 8(2), 6*(1*)
8, 6*, 6(2), 9*(1*)</td><td>6*, 6*, 8*, 9*</td><td>6</td></tr>
<tr><td colspan="5">Comment: Because of the pair of 8's it is much safer for the non-dealer to play one of them as his second card and to score '2 for a pair' than to play his 6 and score 3 points for a sequence and to take the count to '21'. There is little risk of losing points for 'pairs royal' as it would be very unusual for the hands of both players to contain a pair of 8's.</td></tr>
<tr><td>7</td><td>2, 4, 6, 8</td><td>4, 4* (2*), 8, 8* (2*), 6 (1)
6*, 2, 10* (1*)</td><td>4*, 6*, 8*, 10*</td><td>8</td></tr>
<tr><td colspan="5">Comment: If well behind the dealer should take every opportunity of scoring and should pair the lead and risk losing 'pairs royal'. The non-dealer should not play the 6 as the second card in case the dealer's hand contains an (A + 4) combination. Although, in this particular instance, the dealer's play was successful it might have been wiser, if well in the lead, to avoid the risk of losing 'pairs royal' and to play the 8* in reply to the non-dealer's first lead, e.g., [4, 8*, 8(2), 10*(1*)] followed by [6, 6*(2*), 2, 4*(1*)].</td></tr>
</table>

9	A, 3, 4, 10	4, 4*(2*),10, 7*, 3, 2*,A (5)	2*, 4*, 6*, 7*	10
		6* (1*)		

Comment: If well behind, the dealer should pair the lead and risk the loss of 'pairs royal'. Unfortunately, although this is avoided, after playing the 7* as the second card the dealer is obliged to play the 2* which concedes 5 points for a sequence and '31'. If in the lead it might have been wiser not to reply with the 4* and to score '2 for a pair' but to use the 7* instead and hope that the non-dealer had not led from a pair of 4's, for example, [4, 7*, 3, 6*, 10, A (2)] followed by [2*, 4*(1*)].

11	2, 2, 4, 4	4, 9*, 2 (2), 10*, 4, 2 (2)	8*,9*,10*, J*	12
		8*, J* (1*)		

Comment: The dealer should reply with the 9* on the assumption that the non-dealer is more likely to hold either (A + 4) or (3 + 4) than a (2 + 4) combination. Unfortunately the assumption was wrong.

13	2, 3, 10, J	3, 6*, 10, 9*, 2 (1)	4*, 5*, 6*, 9*	14
		4*, J, 5* (1*)		

Comment: It is safer for the non-dealer to lead the 2 or the 3 than to play a '10' card. This results in no change in the relative positions of the players on the cribbage board. The outcome can be very different if the non-dealer leads the 10 or the J, for example, [10, 5* (2*), J, 6* (2*)] followed by [3, 9*, 2, 4* (1*)]. The dealer would gain 5 points.

15	3, 4, 5, 6	4, 3*, 5 (3), 6* (4*), 6 (2), 3*, 3 (3)	3*, 4*, 5*, 6*	16
		5* (1*)		

Comment: The dealer cannot reply to a lead of a 4 by 'playing away' but judges that by playing 3* one sequence can be countered by another rather than pairing the lead with 4* and risking the loss of 'pairs royal'. The 3* is chosen because by playing either the 5* or the 6* might result in the loss of 15/2 as well as a sequence e.g., 4, 5*, 6 (5) and 4, 6*, 5 (5). Even so, by replying with the 3*, the dealer runs the risk of losing 8 points if the cards in the non-dealer's hand had been (2, 4, 5, 7), e.g., [4, 3*, 5 (3), 6* (4*), 2 (5), 4* (5*), 7 (8)]. Alternatively, the dealer might feel that it is worth pairing the lead and to take the risk of the non-dealer having led from a pair of 4's, knowing that the points lost from 'pairs royal' could be partly recouped by making 15/2 with the 3*.

17	8, 9, 10, 10	8, 7* (2*), 9 (3), 7* (2*)	6*, 7*, 7*, 8*	18
		10, 6*, 10 (1) and 8* (1*)		

Comment: By leading the 8 the non-dealer can use the 9 to form a sequence if the dealer is able to reply with a 7* for 15/2. The non-dealer cannot score for a sequence by leading the 9 if the dealer replies with a 6* for 15/2.

19	7, 7, 8, 9	8, 4*, 7, 4*, 7 (1) 6*, 9 (2), 5* (1*)	4*, 4*, 5*, 6*	20
Comment: If the position on the board suggests that caution is sensible the dealer should, with the hand shown in the example, play as illustrated. On the other hand, if well behind and the only chance of winning is by taking risks, different tactics should be used. The dealer should consider playing the 6* in reply to the initial lead and hope that the non-dealer's hand also contains a 7, which is played to make a sequence. The dealer would then be able to continue with the 5* for another sequence and, if the non-dealer was unable to play again, could continue with the 4* for yet another sequence and 'Go' and would gain another 7 points, giving a total of 11 points (4* + 7*) for the whole count, for example, [8, 6*, 7 (3), 5* (4*), 4* (6*)].				
21	6, 7, 7, 8	8, 3*, 7, 2*, 7, A*, A* (3*) 6 (1)	A*, A*,2*,3*	22
Comment: Note the safety play of both players. It is better for the dealer to use the 3* rather than the 2* in reply to the lead because the non-dealer is more likely to hold a 5 than a 4. There is therefore a greater risk of losing 15/2 if the 2* is used in reply.				
23	A, A, 2, 3	2, 2* (2*), A, 3* (3*), 3 (2), 4*, A, 2* (1*)	2*,2*,3*,4*	24
Comment: With a pair of 2's in the hand it is safe for the dealer to pair the lead knowing that, if the non-dealer's hand also contains a pair of 2's and scores one of them for 'pairs royal', the fourth 2 can be played for 'double pairs royal'. Although, in this case this did not happen, the reply from the dealer was also the safest possible. To reply with either the 3* or the 4* would risk a sequence exchange which might be lost.				
25	A, 2, 3, 3	2, 2* (2*), 3, 3* (2*), 3 (6), 3* (12*), A, 2* (4*)	2*, 2*, 3*, 3*	26
Comment: The non-dealer uses one of the pair of 3's in order to score 6 points for 'pairs royal'. Unlucky. The dealer also holds a pair of 3*'s and is able to gain the advantage by scoring 'double pairs royal'. The dealer then scores for a sequence and 'Go' and gains a grand total of 20 points for the whole count, i.e., (2* + 2* + 12*+ 4*).				

Quiz

Five-card cribbage

For each of the following pairs of hands with consecutive numbers decide how to play the cards during pegging. Remember that the first lead belongs to the non-dealer and that there is only one count to 'Go' or '31'. The answers to the quiz are given in the authors' comments in Table 8.2.

#	Non-dealer	Dealer	#	#	Non-dealer	Dealer	#
1	A, 5, 9	5*, 10*, J*	2	3	7, 7, 8	8*, 9*, 10*	4
5	5, 10, K	A*, 5*, 9*	6	7	A, 7, 8	5*, 8*, 10*	8
9	5, 9, 10	6*, 8*, 9*	10	11	7, 8, K	6*, 9*, K*	12
13	6, 7, 8	A*, 2*, 3*	14	15	3, 3, 10	6*, 10*, 10*	16
17	A, A, 8,	4*, 4*, 6*	18	19	8, 8, 10	7*, 7*, 9*	20
21	2, 4, 4	8*, 8*, 10*	22	23	A, 3, 4	A*, 3*, 4*	24
25	A, 6, 7	3*, 6*, 7*	26	27	2, 6, 8	3*, 7*, 9*	28

Answers to quiz

Notes: The same examples are used as in Tables 7.1 to 7.10. The non-dealer has been given the examples with odd numbers and the dealer those with even. The first selection of each example has been used and the scores obtained are shown in brackets. The cards and scores of the dealer have asterisks. The comments are based on how the authors would play these hands. Remember that neither player would have any knowledge of the cards in the other's hand.

Table 8.2 — Scoring by pegging

Five-card cribbage

#	Non-dealer	Cards played and points gained	Dealer	#
1	A, 5, 9	9, 5*, 5 (2), 10*, A (1)	5*, 10*, J*	2
Comment: The non-dealer should lead with the 9 and the dealer should 'play away' with the 5*. Unfortunate. The non-dealer held an (A + 5) combination.				
3	7, 7, 8	7, 8* (2*), 8 (3)	8*, 9*, 10*	4
Comment: The non-dealer should lead from the pair of 7's, hoping to score for 'pairs royal'.				
5	5, 10, K	K, 5* (2*), 5 (2), 9*, A* (1*)	A*, 5*, 9*	6
Comment: The non-dealer should lead the K rather than the 10 and should pair the dealer's reply and risk the loss of 'pairs royal'.				

7	A, 7, 8	8, 8* (2*), A, 10* (1*)	5*. 8*. 10*	8
Comment: The dealer should pair the lead. The non-dealer should reply with the A rather than risk losing a sequence by playing the 7. The dealer should then take the count as high as possible and limit the chance of a further reply from the non-dealer.				
9	5, 9, 10	9, 6* (2*), 10, 6* (2*)	6*, 8*, 9*	10
Comment: It is generally safer to lead a 9 than a 10 because the dealer is more likely to have kept a 5* than a 6*. Unfortunately, in this instance the dealer gained 4 points on the count. Although it would have worked better to have led the 10, a player should not be deflected from best play. If well behind in the game the non-dealer should lead with his 10. Should the dealer's hand contain a 5* and 15/2 is made, the non-dealer can use the 5 to score 2 for a pair, e.g., 10, 5* (2*), 5 (2) etc. and hope to minimise the points lost in the count (see example 5 - 6 above).				
11	7, 8, K	K, K* (2*), 8 (1)	6*, 9*, K*	12
Comment: The non-dealer should reply with the 8 in order to minimise the chance of the dealer scoring for 'Go' or '31'. However, if well behind, it would be better for the non-dealer to lead with the 8 so that, if the dealer's hand contains a 7* and it is played to make 15/2, the 7 can pair it even though it risks the loss of 'pairs royal'.				
13	6, 7, 8	7, 3*, 8, 2*, 6, A* (1*)	A*, 2*, 3*	14
Comment: The non-dealer should lead with the 7 in order to be able to pair the reply if the dealer makes 15/2 by playing an 8*. From the hand shown the dealer should reply with the 3*, taking the view that the other cards in the hand are more likely to help later in the count.				
15	3, 3, 10	3, 6*, 3, 10* (1*)	6*, 10*, 10*	16
Comment: The dealer should not reply with a 10* because (a) the non-dealer may have led from a (2 + 3) combination and (b) if the non-dealer can pair the reply the second of the 10*s could not be used to make 'pairs royal' as the count would exceed '31'. The dealer should therefore reply with the 6* and the non-dealer should counter with the other 3 rather than the greater risk of playing the 10, e.g., 3, 6*, 10, 10* (3*).				
17	A, A, 8	8, 4*, A, 4*, A, 6* (1*)	4*, 4*, 6*	18
Comment: The dealer should reply with a 4* and avoid the risk of giving away a sequence. Because the first 4* was not paired the dealer prefers to play the other 4* rather than the 6* and avoids taking the count to 21.				
19	8, 8, 10	8, 7* (2*), 10 (1)	7*, 7*, 9*	20
Comment. In order to reduce the chance of the dealer playing a second card the non-dealer should use the 10 for his reply and take the count as high as possible. It would be unwise to play the second 8 in case the dealer's hand contained a 6* when 4 points for a sequence and 'Go' would be lost, e.g., 8, 7* (2*), 8, 6* (4*).				

<table>
<tr><td>21</td><td>2, 4, 4</td><td>4, 8*, 4, 10*, 2 (1)</td><td>8*, 8*, 10*</td><td>22</td></tr>
<tr><td colspan="5">Comment: With a lead of a 4 the dealer should reply with the 8* in case the non-dealer has led from an (A + 4) combination. The dealer should use the 10* rather than the second 8* as the second card to make the count as high as possible.</td></tr>
<tr><td colspan="5"></td></tr>
<tr><td>23</td><td>A, 3, 4</td><td>4, 4* (2*), A, A* (2*), 3, 3* (3*)</td><td>A*, 3*, 4*</td><td>24</td></tr>
<tr><td colspan="5">Comment: The dealer should pair the lead rather than risk giving a sequence away.</td></tr>
<tr><td colspan="5"></td></tr>
<tr><td>25</td><td>A, 6, 7</td><td>7, 7*(2*), A (2), 3*, 6, 6* (3*)</td><td>3*, 6*, 7*</td><td>26</td></tr>
<tr><td colspan="5">Comment: With the count at 15 the dealer has to choose whether to use the 3*, and risk losing a sequence, or to use the 6* and take the count to 21 with the risk of the non-dealer's last card being a '10' card.</td></tr>
<tr><td colspan="5"></td></tr>
<tr><td>27</td><td>2, 6, 8</td><td>8, 7* (2*), 6 (3), 9* (5*)</td><td>3*, 7*, 9*</td><td>28</td></tr>
<tr><td colspan="5">Comment: Note the danger the non-dealer runs when forming a sequence with the second card. If in a leading position and wishing to take few risks it would be wiser for the non-dealer to use the 2 as the second card, e.g., 8, 7* (2*), 2, 9*, 3* (1*).</td></tr>
</table>

Chapter 9

ILLUSTRATIVE GAMES

The following complete games of six-card and five-card cribbage have been included to illustrate some points made in the previous chapters. The games are shown in tabular form and, because the deal alternates between the players, the dealer's cards are underlined. The two players in each game are A and B. For easy identification A's cards, and the scores obtained from them, are in italics and B's are shown in bold type. The 'Turn-Up' card is shown with quotation marks. The points scored by both players at each stage are shown in parentheses and shown again on the right-hand side of each Table in columns which, in effect, represent the cribbage board. The authors' comments are given at the end of each deal. To avoid using suit notation in the presentation of the games, it has been assumed that the formation of a flush in any of the hands or cribs was not possible. Neither have any points from 'One for His Nob' and 'Two for His Heels' been included. These and flushes rarely have a major influence on the outcome of a game.

<table>
<tr><th colspan="8">Table 9.1 — Scoring by pegging</th></tr>
<tr><th colspan="8">Six-card two-handed cribbage</th></tr>
<tr><th colspan="8">Player A won the cut and dealt first</th></tr>
<tr><th>Deal</th><th>Cards received by A, selection for hand</th><th>'Turn-Up', order of card play, and crib</th><th>Cards received by B, selection for hand</th><th>A's points during deal</th><th>A's total score</th><th>B's points during deal</th><th>B's total score</th></tr>
<tr><td>1</td><td>2, 3, 7, 9, Q, K</td><td>'4'</td><td>4, 5, 6, 8, J, Q</td><td></td><td></td><td></td><td></td></tr>
<tr><td></td><td></td><td>4, Q, J, 3 (1)</td><td></td><td>1</td><td>1</td><td></td><td></td></tr>
<tr><td></td><td></td><td>6, K, 5, 2 (1)</td><td></td><td>1</td><td>2</td><td></td><td></td></tr>
<tr><td></td><td>2, 3, Q, K (7)</td><td></td><td>4, 5, 6, J (14)</td><td>7</td><td>9</td><td>14</td><td>14</td></tr>
<tr><td></td><td></td><td>7, 8, 9, Q (5)</td><td></td><td>5</td><td>14</td><td></td><td></td></tr>
<tr><td colspan="8">Comment: Both players kept a hand which gave the maximum score without the aid of the 'Turn-Up' card. The card-play by the players was as safe as possible.</td></tr>
<tr><td>2</td><td>A, 6, 7, 10, J, K</td><td>'8'</td><td>3, 3, 8, 10, J, K</td><td></td><td></td><td></td><td></td></tr>
<tr><td></td><td></td><td>7, 8 (2), 6 (3), 10 (2)</td><td></td><td>3</td><td>17</td><td>4</td><td>18</td></tr>
<tr><td></td><td></td><td>J, 3, A, 3 (1)</td><td></td><td></td><td></td><td>1</td><td>19</td></tr>
<tr><td></td><td>A, 6, 7, J (7)</td><td></td><td>3, 3, 8, 10 (4)</td><td>7</td><td>24</td><td>4</td><td>23</td></tr>
<tr><td></td><td></td><td>10, J, K, K (2)</td><td></td><td></td><td></td><td>2</td><td>25</td></tr>
<tr><td colspan="8">Comment: With no score possible from the cards received, the non-dealer (A) kept the selection with the lowest numerical sum, as that this would give the best chance of a score from the 'Turn-Up' card and chose the selection which gave the best discards to the crib. The initial lead of the 7 enabled the non-dealer to counter the 15/2 from the dealer (B) by playing the 6 for 3 points for a sequence knowing that, even if the dealer had a '10' card and scored 2 points for '31', only 1 point would be lost on the full count.</td></tr>
</table>

3	*6, 6, 7, 8, 9, Q*	'5'	**2, 3, 3, 4, 8, 10**				
		3, *8*, **4 (2)**, *7*, **8 (1)**				**3**	**28**
		6, **3**, *6 (3)*		*3*	27		
	6, 6, 7, 8 (12)		**3, 3, 4, 8 (14)**	*12*	*39*	**14**	**42**
		2, *9*, **10**, *Q (4)*		*4*	*43*		
Comment: Both players keep hands giving the maximum score without the aid of the 'Turn-Up' card. The dealer (A) played safe and replied to the initial lead with the 8 and saved the pair of 6's for later in the play. The dealer felt that it was risky to use one of the 6's from the pair and aim for 'pairs royal' in case the non-dealer's hand contained another 6 and a '10' card e.g., **3**, *6*, **6 (4)**, *6 (6)*, **'10' (2)**, when no advantage to either player would have resulted from the full count. In the event the card-play benefited the non-dealer (B).							
4	*A, 3, 4, 8, 9, 9*	'6'	**4, 6, 7, Q, Q, K**				
		4, **4 (2)**, *9*, **Q**, *3 (1)*		*1*	*44*	**2**	**44**
		K, *8*, **Q (1)**				**1**	**45**
	3, 4, 8, 9 (4)		**4, Q, Q, K (2)**	*4*	*48*	**2**	**47**
		A, **6, 7**, *9* **(6)**				**6**	**53**
Comment: A pair of 9's would have been discarded if the non-dealer (A) had kept the selection with the lowest numerical sum as the hand, i.e., *(A, 3, 4, 8)*. The dealer (B) put the best discards into the crib and hoped that the 'Turn-Up' card was either an A or a 5.							
5	*2, 4, 4, 9, 9, Q*	'6'	**A, A, 2, 8, 8, 9**				
		8, *4*, **8**, *9*, **A, A (4)**				**4**	**57**
		2, 4 (1)		*1*	*49*		
	2, 4, 4, 9 (8)		**A, A, 8, 8 (12)**	*8*	*57*	**12**	**69**
		2, 9, *9, Q (6)*		*6*	*63*		
Comment: Both players kept the selections giving the maximum score without the aid of the 'Turn-Up' card. The non-dealer (B) was very lucky that the 'Turn-Up' card was a 6, but it was also beneficial to the score from the crib for the dealer (A).							
6	*2, 2, 5, 7, 8, K*	'A'	**2, 5, 5, 7, 8, 9**				
		2, **2 (2)**, *8*, **8 (2)**, *7 (1)*		*1*	*64*	**4**	**73**
		9, *5*, **7 (1)**				**1**	**74**
	2, 5, 7, 8 (6)		**2, 7, 8, 9 (5)**	*6*	*70*	**5**	**79**
		2, 5, 5, *K* **(6)**				**6**	**85**
Comment: The dealer (B) was able to discard a pair of 5's to the crib and still keep a selection with the maximum guaranteed score from the hand and crib. The non-dealer (A) should have kept *(2, 2, 5, 8)* as the hand, which scores the maximum without the aid of the 'Turn-Up' card, and discarded the *7* and *K* to the crib.							

7	*2, 5, 8, 8, 9, Q*	'3'	**A, 3, 4, 7, 9, Q**				
		7, *8 (2)*, **4**, *9*, **3 (2)**		2	72	**2**	**87**
		8, **A**, *2 (1)*		1	73		
	2, 8, 8, 9 (2)		**A, 3, 4, 7 (6)**	2	75	**6**	**93**
		5, **9**, *Q*, **Q** *(6)*		6	81		
Comment: By choosing the hand shown and discarding the *(5, Q)* to the crib (an overall guaranteed score of 4 points), the dealer (A) judged that the 2 points lost by not keeping *(2, 5, 8, 8)* as the hand (a guaranteed score of 6 points), would be recovered via the 'Turn-Up' card and the discards by the non-dealer (B).							
8	*4, 6, 9, 9, J, K*	'2'	**A, 3, 6, 6, 10, Q**				
		9, **6 (2)**, *9*, **6**, **A (2)**				**4**	**97**
		4, **3**, *6 (1)*		1	82		
	4, 6, 9, 9 (10)		**A, 3, 6, 6 (9)**	10	92	**9**	**106**
		10, *J*, **Q**, *K* **(4)**				**4**	**110**
Comment: The non-dealer (A) would have been wiser to have kept *(6, 9, 9, J)* and discarded *(4, K)*. It would also have been better to use the *6* as the initial lead so that, if the dealer (B) was able to reply with a **9** for 15/2, the 2 points lost could be recovered with the other *9* from the pair, knowing that there could be no risk of the loss of 6 points for 'pairs royal' because the count would have reached 24.							
9	*5, 8, 8, 10, Q, Q*	'10'	**A, 2, 3, 9, J, J**				
		J, *5 (2)*, **J**, **3**, **2 (1)**		2	94	**1**	**111**
		10, Q, Q (3)		3	97		
	5,10,Q, Q (12)		**2, 3, J, J (8)**	12	109	**8**	**119**
		A, *8, 8*, **9** *(8)*		8	117		
Comment: The 'Turn-Up' card was particularly helpful to the dealer (A). At the end of this deal both players know that the next deal was almost certainly the last of the game and was likely to be settled by the points pegged during card play.							
10	*4, 5, 8, 9, 9, Q*	'7'	**A, 2, 6, 7, J, K**				
		4, **7**, *9*, **6**, *5 (2)*		2	119		
		2, *8*, **A (1)**				1	**120**
	4, 5, 8, 9 (5)		**A, 2, 6, 7 (8)**	5	*win*		
		9, **J**, *Q*, **K (3)**					
Comment: Thinking that the scores from the hands and the crib would be irrelevant to the outcome of the game both players kept a hand which was most likely to score by pegging. The non-dealer (A) used the 4 as a 'safe' lead and the dealer (B) replied with the 7, judging that a reply with the 6 might result in the game being lost, for example, (*4*, **6**, *5* (5)). In the event player (B) lost the game anyway but, surprisingly, the score from (A), the non-dealer's hand was required.							

Table 9.2 — Scoring by pegging

Five-card two-handed cribbage

Player A won the cut and dealt first. Player B pegged 'three for last'.

Deal	Cards received by A, selection for hand	'Turn-Up', order of card play, and crib	Cards received by B, selection for hand	A's points during deal	A's total score	B's Points during deal	B's total score
1	2, 3, 6, 9, K	'7'	**2, 3, 4, 8, J**			**3**	**3**
		4, K, **3**, 3 (2), **2**, 2 (3)		5	5		
	2, 3, K (2)		**2, 3, 4 (3)**	2	7	**3**	**6**
		6, **8**, 9, **J** (8)		8	15		
Comment: Both players kept selections giving the maximum score. The non-dealer (B) chose the 4 as a safe lead and the dealer (A), in order to play away, was forced to reply with the K and risk the possibility that the non-dealer had led from an (A + 4) combination.							
2	*4, 5, 9, 10, J*	'3'	**A, 4, 6, 9, 10**				
		10, **10 (2)**, *J*, **A (2)**				**4**	**10**
	5, 10, J (4)		**A, 4, 10 (2)**	*4*	*19*	**2**	**12**
		4, 6, *9*, **9 (6)**				**6**	**18**
Comment: Despite the risk of the possible loss of 'pairs royal' the dealer (B) decided to pair the lead. In this instance the play was successful, but it would have been safer to reply with the 4, knowing that if the non-dealer (A) had led from an (A + 4) combination and played the A for 15/2, the points could be recovered by pairing that A.							
3	*A, 2, 3, 4, 9*	'2'	**4, 5, 7, 8, 8**				
		8, *4*, **8**, *3*, **7 (1)**			*19*	**1**	**19**
	2, 3, 4 (8)		**7, 8, 8 (6)**	*8*	*27*	**6**	**25**
		A, **4, 5**, *9 (4)*		*4*	*31*		
Comment: By discarding a 5 to the dealer's crib the non-dealer (B) was guaranteed 6 points from the hand. Any other selection only guaranteed 2 points.							
4	*A, 4, 4, Q, K*	'8'	**2, 3, 7, 9, 9**				
		4, **9**, *4*, **9**, *A (1)*		*1*	32		
	A, 4, 4 (2)		**7, 9, 9 (10)**	*2*	34	**10**	**35**
		2, 3, *Q, K* **(4)**				**4**	**39**
Comment: The non-dealer (A) could only score 2 points with any selection from the cards received. By keeping the selection shown it was hoped that the 'Turn-Up' card would be a '10' card and that the low cards in the hand would score points by pegging. Neither was successful. The dealer (B) was able to discard a (2 + 3) combination to the crib and both the 'Turn-Up' card and the non-dealer's discards were beneficial to the selection chosen.							

5	A, 2, 5, 8, 9	'9'	A, 5, 5, 6, 9				
		6, 9 (2), 5, 8, A (1)		1	36		
	A, 8, 9 (2)		5, 5, 6 (4)	2	38	4	43
		A, 2, 5, 9 (6)		6	44		

Comment: The dealer could have kept either (2, 5, 8) or (A, 5, 9) as the hand, both scoring 2 points without the aid of the 'Turn-Up' card, but decided to discard the 5 with the hope of obtaining a large score from the crib. The non-dealer (B) was able to keep the pair of 5's in hand.

6	A, 3, 6, 9, 9	'5'	5, 5, 6, 8, J				
		9, 6 (2), 9, 6 (1)		1	45	2	45
	6, 9, 9 (6)		6, 8, J (2)	6	51	2	47
		A, 3, 5, 5 (8)				8	55

Comment: The non-dealer (A) had to discard the (A + 3) combination in order to keep the guaranteed score of 6 points from the hand. The dealer (B) decided on a hand with no guaranteed score and hoped that the pair of 5's would provide a large score from the crib. During the card play the non-dealer did not pair the dealer's 6 because of the risk of losing either 'pairs royal' or '31'.

7	2, 4, J, Q, K	'K'	A, 3, 4, 8, 9				
		4, K, 8, 3 (1)				1	56
	J, Q, K (8)		3, 4, 8 (2)	8	59	2	58
		A, 2, 4, 9 (4)		4	win		

Comment: The dealer (A) judged that neither player was likely to win by pegging and that it was best to aim for the maximum score from the hand and the crib. The non-dealer (B) calculated that, in order to win, 2 points were required by pegging and the 'Turn-Up' card needed to be either an 8 or a 3 or a 4. The 'Turn-Up' was kind to the dealer.

Appendix 1

GLOSSARY

Balking the Crib	To discard with the least likely advantage to the dealer.
Box	An alternative name for the crib.
Court Cards	King, Queen and Jack. Also known as face cards. All have the numerical value of 10.
Discard	A card placed into the crib.
Discarding	The act of selecting cards from those received at each deal and of placing them, face-down, into the crib.
'Double Lurch'	To defeat the opponent by 61 or more points in a single game. The winner scores four games.
Double Pairs Royal	Four cards of the same rank.
Face Cards	King, Queen and Jack. Also known as court cards.
Fifteen-Two (15/2)	Any combination of cards with the numerical sum equal to 15.
Flush	All of the cards retained in the hand are of one suit or all of the cards in the crib and the 'Turn-Up' card are of one suit.
Game Hole	The end of the game. The 121st hole in two-handed six-card cribbage and the 61st hole in two-handed five-card cribbage.
'Go'	Neither player can play a card without the sum of the cards exceeding 31.
'Lurch'	To defeat the opponent by 31 or more points in a single game. The winner scores two games.
Mud Hole	The last but one hole in a game of cribbage.
'Muggins'	The term given to a player who fails to claim part of his score. The opponent can then claim the underscore.
'One for his Nob'	One extra point for having the jack of the same suit as the 'Turn-Up' card.
Pair	Two cards of the same rank.
Pairs Royal	Three cards of the same rank.
Pegging	The act of scoring the points gained by using small pegs and a cribbage board.
Rank	The numerical value of an individual card.
Run	Three or more cards in adjacent numerical order. The cards need not be of the same suit.
Salting the Crib	To discard with the most likely advantage to the dealer.
Sequence	The same as run.
Score	The number of points that a player has made towards game.
Shuffled	All the cards have been thoroughly mixed together.
'Skunk'	Having the same meaning as lurch.
Starter Card	The card turned face-up after the pack has been cut. Also called the 'Turn-Up' card.
Suit	A set of thirteen cards of one kind, that is, clubs, diamonds, hearts or spades, consisting of one of each of the following cards: Ace, 2, 3, 4, 5, 6, 7, 8, 9, 10, jack, queen, king.
'Ten' Cards	All the kings, queens, jacks and tens.
Thirty-one ('31')	The sum of the cards played is equal to 31.
'Turn-Up' card	The card turned face-up after the pack has been cut. Also 'Starter Card'.
'Two for His Heels'	Two points, scored by the dealer, if the 'Turn-Up' card is a jack.

Appendix 2

THE LAWS OF CRIBBAGE

1. The cards must be cut to decide which player is the first to deal. The first cut must consist of at least four cards and must not remove more than half the pack. The player cutting last must leave at least four cards in the remainder of the pack.

2. The player cutting the lowest card deals first. Ace is the lowest and the King the highest card with the other cards ranking in sequence. Players must cut again if they cut cards of the same rank.

3. If more than one game is played the starting deal should alternate between the players.

4. Throughout each game the players should deal alternately.

5. Before each game the cards should be shuffled with each player having the right to do so. However, the dealer should be the last to shuffle them.

6. The non-dealer should then cut the pack of cards in two and should place the top packet alongside the bottom packet. The non-dealer should not look at the bottom card of the top packet but, if this happens, the dealer can claim 2 penalty points and the cards should then be picked up, shuffled and cut again.

7. The dealer should then place the bottom packet on top of the top packet, pick up the cards and deal them, one at a time, starting with the non-dealer.

8. No penalty is invoked if the dealer exposes one of his own cards during the deal.

9. 2 points are lost if the dealer exposes one of the opponent's cards. Also, as long as the rest of the cards have not been looked at, the non-dealer can demand a fresh deal.

10. 2 points are lost if the non-dealer exposes one of the cards before the deal has been completed. The dealer also has the option of a fresh deal.

11. 2 points are lost by the dealer if too many cards are dealt to either player. For the points to be claimed, the non-dealer must notice the error before picking up the cards. Irrespective of whether the points are claimed or not, the dealer must deal again.

12. 2 points are lost by the dealer if too few cards are dealt to either player. The non-dealer also has the option, after looking at the cards, of either demanding a fresh deal or of completing the hand from the top of the pack.

13. If a card is face-up in the pack whilst the cards are being dealt there must be a fresh deal.

14. When the wrong player has dealt the cards there must be a fresh deal if the error is discovered before the rest of the pack is cut for the 'Turn-Up' card. The deal must stand if the error is not discovered until after the 'Turn-Up' card has been seen.

15. If, discarding to the crib, a player is found by the opponent to have had too many cards and has not declared the error, the opponent scores 2 points and has the option of either demanding a fresh deal or of accepting the deal that was in error. If the latter is chosen the opponent has the right of withdrawing the extra card (or cards) from the offender's hand and of looking at it (them) before returning it (them) to the pack.

16. The non-dealer must discard to the crib before the dealer does. Cards placed into the crib cannot be returned to the hand.
17. A player scores 2 points if the opponent takes back into the hand a card that had been discarded to the crib. The player also has the option of a fresh deal.
18. The crib must not be touched until after the cards have been played and the counts from the hands recorded. Only the dealer is entitled to touch the crib.
19. When cutting for the 'Turn-Up' card the non-dealer must take at least four cards from the top and leave at least four cards at the bottom of the pack.
20. If the dealer turns over more than one card the non-dealer may choose which of them shall be the 'Turn-Up' card.
21. If the 'Turn-Up' card is a jack the dealer scores 2 points for 'His Heels'. These points are forfeited if the dealer plays the first card before they are pegged on the board. It does not matter if the non-dealer has already made the first lead.
22. A player forfeits 2 points if, during the play of the cards, he announces 'Go' but has a card that can be played without the sum exceeding 31.
23. There is no penalty if, during the play of the cards, either player incorrectly states the sum of the cards played.
24. If a player records more points than is justified, either as the cards are played or when the counts are made from the hand and crib, the total score shall be reduced by the number of points over-scored. By way of penalty the opponent shall add the same number of points to his own score.
25. If a player fails to score points to which entitled either when scoring the hand or crib, or as a result of a penalty, the opponent may claim the points which have been overlooked.
26. A player must announce and peg the score from the hand and crib without any assistance from the opponent. The cards in the hand and crib must be laid out so that the opponent is able to check that the points claimed are correct.
27. If both of a player's pegs are accidentally displaced the opponent must replace them.
28. If a leading peg is displaced by accident it should be returned to the hole from which it was displaced or, when there is uncertainty, to a hole that is mutually agreeable to both players.
29. A player cannot, without the permission of the opponent, alter points that have just been pegged. If too many have been pegged the opponent should invoke Law 25 above.
30. A player forfeits the points for the hand and/or crib if they have not been pegged before the cards are picked up for the next deal.
31. A player forfeits all the points in the hand and/or crib if the cards are mixed together or with the remainder of the pack before those points have been pegged.
32. A player forfeits the game if any penalty incurred is not paid.
33. The game is forfeit if a player moves a peg into the 'end-hole' in error.

PENALTY POINTS

The manner in which penalty points are awarded are summarised in the Table opposite. The rules covering 'Lurch' and 'Muggins' are also included in this section although, strictly speaking, they are not penalties arising from deliberate or accidental errors. In these cases the 'penalty' accrued by the recipient is due either to bad luck or to incompetence when playing the cards.

'Muggins'

If, when a player announces the score from either the hand or the crib and overlooks some of the points available, the opponent should say 'Muggins' and should score the number of points which were overlooked.

The 'Lurch' or The 'Skunk'

When, in two-handed six-card cribbage, one player scores 121 before the opponent has scored 91, the winner counts the result as a *double game*. Some cribbage boards have a line just after the 90th hole, which is known as the 'lurch' or 'skunk' line. In two-handed five-card cribbage the lurch line is 31 and the winner counts the result as a *double game* when scoring 61 before the opponent reaches the lurch line.

The 'Double Lurch' or The 'Double Skunk'

This occurs very rarely and applies when in two-handed six-card cribbage one player scores 121 before the opponent reaches 61. The winner thereby scores *four games*.

Table of Penalty Points

Offending Action	*Penalty claimed by dealer*	*Penalty claimed by non-dealer*	*Law*
Non-dealer looks at bottom card of top packet of cards as they are cut	2 points		6
Dealer exposes one of opponent's cards		2 points	9
Non-dealer exposes a card before deal is completed	2 points		10
Dealer deals too many cards (non-dealer must discover error before picking cards up)		2 points	11
Dealer deals too few cards (non-dealer can, after looking at the cards, either claim a fresh deal or take additional cards from the top of the stockpile)		2 points	12
Either player has too many cards in the hand after discarding	2 points	2 points	15
Either player takes back a card into the hand from the crib.	2 points	2 points	17
Either player announces 'Go' when another card could have been played	2 points	2 points	22
Either player records more points than justified. The total shall be reduced by the overscore which shall be added to the score of the opponent	– or + the overscore	– or + the overscore	24
Either player has not pegged all the points before the cards are picked up for the next deal	Score forfeited	Score forfeited	25
Dealer mixes hand and crib before pegging the score	Score forfeited	Score forfeited	30
Either player mixes cards with the rest of the pack before pegging the score	Score forfeited	Score forfeited	31
Either player fails to pay a penalty	Game forfeited	Game forfeited	32
Either player moves a peg into the end-hole in error	Game forfeited	Game forfeited	33